TRAUMA–SENSITIVE MOVEMENT

96 SOMATIC TECHNIQUES
to Support Nervous System Regulation and Embodied Transformation in Therapy

Manuela Mischke-Reeds, MA, MFT

Published by
PESI Publishing, Inc.
3839 White Ave
Eau Claire, WI 54703

Cover design by Amy Rubenzer
Interior design by Emily Dyer
Editing by Marisa Solis

ISBN 9781683738114 (print)
ISBN 9781683738121 (ePUB)
ISBN 9781683738138 (ePDF)

PESI Publishing
pesipublishing.com

TABLE OF CONTENTS

INTRODUCTION

"What we call 'body' is not matter but movement. [...] The 'body' is a profound orchestration of many qualities and textures of movement—interpenetrating tones of fertile play waiting to be incubated. What I see as 'body' is the movement of creative flux, waves of fertility. The cosmic play that we carry into this atmosphere still intrinsically pulsates."

—Emilie Conrad, *Life on Land*

Movement is a gateway to the innate wisdom that dwells deep in our soma. The moving body, therefore, is a pathway to an embodied experience of our life. Movement is, after all, our first language. A tilt of the head, twitch in a foot, curl of an upper lip, shrinking of a chest, wave of a finger—these are the vocabulary of a feeling, sensing, breathing, *moving* language.

Indeed, these are behaviors but they're also expressions of conscious and unconscious emotions, thoughts, sensations, and memories. According to communications experts, up to 80 percent of our communication is nonverbal. So why are we relying on mostly spoken communication in the therapy room?

Because movement is what we are, we don't realize that movement is a pathway of knowing ourselves. As therapists, we can learn to read this nonverbal language of movement to understand what is beneath our clients' stories. Movement can be a diagnostic and therapeutic tool we can use to intervene and help regulate a trauma activation or facilitate working through a stuck emotion. It can be something we utilize to explore, lead, mirror, and join.

As the unspoken language of the unconscious, movement in therapy takes somatic resourcing a step farther. It takes trauma-informed care to the level of teaching concrete tools for self-regulation. By helping a client access and process what is held in their body, we move toward transformation and healing more effectively than talk therapy alone. We know that unprocessed trauma memories dwell in the body. The memories are held and expressed in posture, eye gaze, gesture, tone of voice, cellular memory. This is why movement therapy is a profound and effective way to communicate with what is not known inside and help process it.

Who This Book Is For

Trauma-Sensitive Movement is designed to help any therapist wanting to skillfully use movement as an intervention. I've written it for the beginner therapist who is curious about bringing movement into their practice, the experienced therapist who wants to build out their repertoire for treating trauma, and the somatic psychotherapist who isn't getting consistent results with clients, particularly those with very expressive dispositions.

If you've had a client who had a movement—fidgeting or tremor or tension around the mouth, as just a few examples—and you didn't know what to do with that movement, this book is for you. You'll learn, for example, how to notice the subtle shaking in your client's shoulder, and then how to intervene and facilitate working through it. You'll know that this movement may show you a direct route to unconsciously held material and unprocessed trauma material. You'll experience a kind of psychospiritual process because movement work is like opening a mystery. Once we move, we don't know what will come next—and nothing is static. That is profound learning for trauma clients who are stuck in the trauma past. You'll learn how to read a moving body, and you'll be able to help your client learn to move with and beyond the trauma story.

You will learn:

- Why it is important to include movement in psychotherapy

- How language can facilitate the moving body in session

- How to offer tools that explore both expressive and intrinsic movement

- How to access deeper internalized themes by reading nonverbal movement cues

- How to use and adapt movement tools in clinical practice

- Ways to work with both low- and high-activation trauma states

- How to integrate breath and sound with movement

- How to become attuned to developmental movement in therapy

- Ways to co-regulate through moving together with your client

- How to bring sensitivity to working with the compromised or pained body

How This Book Can Help Your Clients

The most profound offering this book extends is a shift in perspective: to see movement as an inner technology, a precise intervention to help clients work with trauma states, rather than simply as a function, behavior, or expression. Within these pages you'll find education, tools, worksheets, and exercises—both therapist-guided and self-guided—that will help you to see through movement's eyes. The exercises offer deep and exploratory embodiment practices for your clients to feel regulated and safe in their bodies. To be regulated and in touch with the moving body is in itself a resource.

This workbook offers a cross-disciplinary approach integrating trauma-informed movement and somatic psychotherapy. The techniques, philosophies, practices, and tools are inspired by dance therapy, movement practices, expressive arts therapy, somatic psychology, and trauma-informed psychotherapy. You will be teaching your clients to come into relationship with their innate somatic wisdom, to profoundly connect with a tool they always have with them. You will help them explore through their sensing, feeling, and moving body toward wholeness and the insight that dwells deep in their soma.

In the trauma field, there's a large emphasis on "soothe and settle," which is critical in establishing internal safety. What is less practiced is how to integrate the whole spectrum of our movement expressions.

Big expressive emotions that are not easily soothed or settled need a different engagement, as do subtle intrinsic movements. The key is reading the body as *being* movement itself and learning how to meet the client's range of expression. We can learn to read what the client needs and tailor exercises to work with the moving body as a gateway into emotions and deeply held beliefs. As a movement therapist, you will notice and somatically attune to what inside the client wants to move, facilitate a safe expression, and not impose any agenda.

When we ignore movement in our clients or don't leverage movement as a therapeutic tool, we can miss out on a range of opportunities for interventions:

- We can miss the fullness of the client's experience.

- We can miss an important avenue of communication, particularly if a client tends to be nonverbal or in a trauma-activated state.

- We can misread or dismiss body language cues.

- By staying in a cognitive, solutions-focused orientation, our client loses out on shifting into a somatic-focused orientation for an embodied transformation.

- Not knowing how to intervene with clients who are very kinesthetic can lead them to feel not understood—essentially a language mismatch. When we don't understand movement, we don't understand a part of human language. It's as simple as that.

- Finally, if we choose not to work with movement, we can miss out on play and social connection as a profound healing component of trauma therapy. Joy, laughter, creativity, and play are very important aspects of our human emotional and social connection. I've never laughed so much with a client as when we were rolling around on the floor in childlike delight, discovering the ease in their body or deeply held feelings released through their body. These moments of shared experience are building blocks in the therapeutic progression. These are underused neural pathways to healing that movement in therapy prioritizes.

Approach this book as a guide and toolbox for your clinical practice. As in many somatic explorations, be a keen observer of what is true for your client. The exercises will help you to explore the somatic movement patterns in the body, allowing clients to get relief from trauma states and find new living resources. They will also strengthen clients' internal knowledge and confidence. Use these exercises to help your clients work with trauma states in creative and gentle ways. Some are about regulating, and some are about exploring deeper themes that want to be released. Each tool has a purpose assigned to it; use your creativity and adjust the exercise for your individual client's needs to fulfill that purpose. All the exercises are in the service of the client learning to trust their own somatic moving intelligence. These are tools for self-discovery and helping you as the clinician to deepen your somatic toolkit.

Navigating the Tools

In this book you will find several icons that indicate for whom the tool is designed:

 Client exercise or tool: These are worksheets or self-guided exercises for your clients, which you might assign as homework after a session. I suggest that you practice these with your client first, so that you can modify them to your client's needs.

 Therapist-guided exercise: These are meant to only be used in the therapy work together, as you will guide the client through the exercise or be an active part of it. This is particularly important when you are working on attachment themes, relational trauma, or developmental themes in therapy. These movement tools can be helpful aids in your work.

 Therapist tool or exercise: These are tools or exercises designed for you as the therapist. They are meant to help you train more in utilizing movement and support your process and your role.

Within the interventions, you will find ready-made **therapist scripts** that you can read aloud to guide your client through the steps. The scripts are meant to be suggestions, so improvise as needed and per your client. This book also offers **journaling prompts**, typically as part of the reflection component of the exercises. Many of the exercises integrate writing as an important resourcing and consolidating element.

My Movement Story

Movement has been my lifelong teacher of what it means to be embodied. During my formative child and teen years I studied many dance forms, from ballet to modern to African dance with a teacher from the musician lineage of the griots of Senegal. I performed, choreographed, and taught movement to children, teens, and adults and saw how bodies in movement would undergo a deep transformative journey. These early teaching experiences set me on a learning journey to understand what it is about movement that heals. My quest brought me to train in dance movement therapy, Continuum Movement®, Authentic Movement, Body-Mind Centering®, Tamalpa Institute methodologies, somatic psychology, yoga, bodywork, Hakomi therapy, Somatic Experiencing®, embodied meditation, internal family systems (IFS), eye movement desensitization and reprocessing (EMDR), and psychedelic-assisted therapies. I was filling my cup with many modalities—and then one day, I could no longer move anymore.

I was a newly minted somatic psychotherapist and had been working with head trauma patients and political torture survivors, after which I had a crisis. I was impacted by the suffering I was witnessing—the pain that I was seeing in the trauma bodies was overwhelming. I observed the heavy emotional burden of the racialized body with my clients and students. I started to move less and began to lose my connection with my own moving intelligence. The more I helped others, the less I filled my own moving cup. At that time, applying movement as the actual inherent wisdom to help metabolize the trauma states was not fully recognized.

I started to practice movement in nature, inviting students to experiment with movements in bodies of water, among trees and forests. I guided students to sense the natural world through their moving bodies in the spaciousness of wind, the liquid teachings of water, and the steadiness of earth. In my experience, this was the ultimate therapy room. Held in reciprocity with the elements, our bodies would find restorative pathways back to oneself.

What I had found inside myself, with students and in nature, I brought back into the therapy room. Clients began to move and connect with their innate impulses into sacred inner experiences.

My trauma clients would move calmly through their anxiety; heavy emotional states would transform. Micro-motion within the body had a big internal impact on the nervous system and connected clients with a collective sense of belonging.

Continuum Movement became a central bridge of principles and practices into my trauma work. These intrinsic movement practices were based on the biological model of how the body moves, like water.

At the same time, I studied Somatic Experiencing with Peter Levine and the Hakomi method, and saw a natural connection between innate movement work, mindful sensing, and trauma-resolution techniques. Stephen Porges's polyvagal theory taught me the importance of safe therapeutic tuning to the underlying rhythms of the body's ventral vagal healing. I experimented with intrinsic movement exploration for clients and students when they touched into trauma states, knowing that the body's natural and organismic movements would initiate the parasympathetic and ventral vagal capacity. I saw big shifts in how they related to their trauma experiences. The capacity for sensing the body in safety and, at the same time, staying in a relationship with their present experience was evident. The impulse to connect with the whole-self, dwelling deep in the clients' soma, came alive, and they began to open to connection, trust, and belonging.

Since that formative experience as a therapist, there have been many times when I stood still and could not move anymore. I always took it as a sign that some new learning was emerging, that I needed to tune into the stillness that not moving brings. Deep listening to one's soma and tuning into the movement qualities on the ends of the spectrum need to be honored. It took me decades to decipher the inner and outer movements of my life, understanding my privileged white, bicultural European, able-bodied experience along with the immigrant experience of my childhood in my native country and my chosen immigrant life in the US. My somatic mover was always a refuge, a pathway, and a deep resource throughout my own traumas, guiding me to wisdom.

Moving Beyond

Movement is many things, from playful to a deep spiritual unfolding. Even when we are constricted, less able, or afraid to move, the innate forward motion of our biology is a basic life form that we can connect with. Find out for yourself what movement means: go out in nature; move with the trees, the wind, and the water; watch how fire dances. Observe the beauty and grace in everyone's body as they move around.

Movement is also a tool that unearths a deep and profound connection to our well-being and healing. It's my hope that you will feel courageous and confident in trying out the exercises in this book with your client. Tap into your therapeutic intelligence and training—and your relational reading of each client situation—and you will transform your sessions into whole-body healing.

Practice compassion for the clients who have not yet found a way back to this innate wisdom, and bring a little (or a lot of) creativity when figuring out which tools work for each client. These are practices known by all of us, deep in the soma. Or as the famous dancer Isadora Duncan once said, "Dance is the movement of the universe concentrated in an individual." Discover and enjoy the universe within.

CHAPTER 1

WHY BRING MOVEMENT INTO THERAPY?

"I move, therefore I am."

—Haruki Murakami, *1Q84*

We are movement. Our heart beats every moment, pulsing blood and life force through our body. The fluids in our body move, in tandem with our breath, through the rivers of our inner systems. The cell structure of our internal architecture expands and collapses with the rise and fall of our rhythmic breathing. Breath is the principal mover, sending tides of waves through the entire body with each breath cycle. We are moving even at rest, even when we appear to be still at first—yet even then, stillness, to the trained eye, is a type of movement.

We tend not to think about movement very consciously throughout our regular day, unless we do so from a functional or behavioral perspective. For example, we reach for a glass of water when we're thirsty, we do physical exercise to release stress. In other words, we think of movement as something that we *do*, not something that we *are*.

But if we shift our perspective to seeing movement as what we *are*, this can vastly change the way we approach treating trauma in therapy. Movement, then, is not just emotional expression; it's something with which to engage, intervene, connect, dialogue, explore, and more.

Nonverbal Inner Worlds

"The conscious mind penetrates unconscious and unexpressed areas of the body, awakening awareness in the body and integrating body and mind into a coherent whole."

—Linda Hartley, *Somatic Psychology*

Movement is *the* language in which we communicate nonverbally. In fact, it is our earliest form of communication. Our moving body in utero moves with the sounds and motions and heartbeat of our mother. The movement of the breath is our first connection with life ex utero. We are born into a relationship with movement. All our relations on this planet are moving relationships—they are dynamic exchanges of nonverbal communication, breath, and vocalizations.

Preverbal babies signal their needs with innate, primal movements. Children navigate our world by mirroring the movements of those around them. Adults express emotional states through hand gestures, facial expressions, and body posture. We might withdraw or shrink our body, communicating that we're overwhelmed by a too fast-paced environment. We might relax into our body, ease our breath, and communicate that we feel safe. We respond to the gentle movement of a caressing hand on our arm as well as to a harsh touch. Though the impact of the quality of these contacts is different, they are both rooted in the sensory perceptions of our body. We communicate through our moving body all the time.

A touching story from a Virginia zoo illustrates how we learn and relate through movement. A mother orangutan at the zoo was unable to breastfeed her newborn. Many attempts were made to teach the new mom maternal instincts, through videos and having zookeepers carry stuffed animals on their bellies. But none of it worked until a zookeeper who also happened to be a breastfeeding mother sat in front of the orangutan and showed her how she breastfed her baby. Within 24 hours the orangutan not only began to breastfeed, but she also cared for and tended to her newborn more appropriately (Metro Richmond Zoo, 2023).

From a movement perspective, we can say that this mother needed to see the behavior and movement of how caring for a newborn is done. An orangutan in captivity is a traumatized being, unable to learn and thrive through the natural environment and another orangutan. We mirror through movement, the unspoken language of how to behave. Mirror neurons fire in synchrony when we see others model a behavior. When we are deprived of these unspoken learnings, we miss a whole vocabulary of how to interact and thrive.

We take for granted that we are moving through the world. We don't usually think about our moving body unless we are injured or impaired in some way. We simply move. We are constantly moving mammals, and in that moving we learn, assess our surroundings for safety, and seek out connection and emotional thriving.

Further, reading movements in others is hardwired into our autonomic nervous system. We must learn to read others accurately and assess if we are in danger or safe—in milliseconds. We learn to intuit facial expressions, body posture, and other qualities of movements. We adjust to others through distancing or approaching movements depending on whether we want to gain space or be close.

For example, when someone is moving toward us with speed, hunched shoulders, a grimacing face, and clenched fists, we will automatically respond with impulses to flee, freeze, or ready ourselves to defend. We don't need a verbal explanation of why or what is happening. Our body—our nervous system specifically—will read the person's movement as a threat and we'll act toward safety. However, if a person is moving toward us with an open, relaxed posture and a bright smile, this will elicit a very different response: perhaps joy, elation, or a sense of excitement. We interpret movement—of others' and our own bodies—to know if we need to connect or disconnect.

Interestingly, we are often not conscious of this intelligence residing in us. So very much is communicated nonverbally, through movement—and yet this profound and sensitive tool we all possess goes unused, particularly in the therapy room, when it stands to make deep, transformational change in our clients. As clinicians we don't commonly and sensitively pay attention to how we can utilize this powerful and unconscious language of the body for the client to self-discover and learn about their own expressions. Let's change that with this book.

Movement in Therapy

"Our body is a source of truth."

—**Albert Pesso**, "Introduction to Pesso System/Psychomotor"

Bringing movement to therapy is a potent tool for self-awareness. One way this happens is when the client is invited to slow down and explore their experience through movement. Simple instructions such as "How is this feeling of excitement right now expressed in your movement?" connect the sensing, feeling, and moving body. This direct experience helps the client understand not only their patterns but also their potentials. It can bring greater connection with their self and with others.

For trauma clients in particular, movement becomes an invaluable tool to release and move trauma responses and restore nervous system function. Connecting with the moving body gets us back in touch with a deep sense of regulated, calm, and safe connection with the goodness of our body. Movement can also be used to assess where a client is on the trauma-response physiological continuum.

In addition, movement uncovers psychological themes, holds memories, and gives an outlet to express feelings that can't be spoken. Moving first, processing, and then talking is a sequence I prefer as a clinician. It allows the thinking and fear-driven mind to calm and lifts the cloudiness of faulty perceptions and assumptions.

In working with movement, a client may realize, for example, that their fast-moving arm is their body's way of pushing for a boundary in a relationship—a relationship that the client is seeing for the first time as oppressed. A client might come to realize that their stiff torso with a frozen feeling inside is a symptom of how much they hold back and suppress their natural expression. Your client's twitching foot, when you pay attention, might signal an underlying nervousness and a yearning to escape a painful feeling that is sitting deep within. In therapy, the words often follow the movement expression. Your client will need to feel and physicalize before they can understand themselves.

But unless we train the clinical eye toward understanding the unspoken movement language, we can't intervene accurately. Many therapists have the mistaken belief that movement is only behavior. As such, we may categorize movement as a personality trait or a quirky expression. Or we may assume what a movement means. We may miss the royal road to the unconscious belief the client could be connecting with. The body moves because it wants to communicate what it feels and yearns for—and we as therapists should investigate that.

We can only find out what a movement means when we connect it with the interest of the client. We must skillfully unravel the mysterious language of movement because these movements have meaning and are avenues to explore in the therapy itself. Movement coupled with conscious awareness in the therapeutic container has the capacity to transform deeply held trauma patterns in the body. This is beyond releasing tremors and unprocessed trauma responses, which is essential. In these moments, the client feels and senses their way through the inner landscapes of mixed feelings and confusing sensations. Movement sorts it all out without the need for verbalization or explanation. Movement begins to metabolize that which would not be understood consciously. Trauma, we can say, can't be fully comprehended but movement can help process it.

In the therapeutic container, we need to set that intention to explore movement as a gateway into the soulfulness of what is truly beneath. When we bring movement into therapy, we invite:

- How the client is using their movements to communicate with others
- How they experience themselves in the physical therapeutic space
- How they experience the therapeutic relationship
- How they can become aware of their own moving body for expression and healing

PSYCHEDELIC-ASSISTED APPLICATION

This approach also applies to psychedelic-assisted therapy, where movement can be quite helpful. In psychedelic-assisted therapy, you will need specific tools that are nonverbal and nondirective. You need tools that support the client's intelligence of their body. In many ways, when working with movement, we must learn to see the body differently, read the body more accurately, tuning into the internal state of the client versus applying a preset prescription. We shift our perceptions from application to invitation.

When practices such as those in this book are repeated, research teaches us, we gain new skills that we begin to internalize. In the beginning, for your client, it will feel new, like a discovery. But with repetition, your client will begin to learn about their somatic inner landscape through which they can ground themselves. Over time and with making these exercises practices, they will begin to truly see the power: when under stress, when a trauma trigger resurfaces, they can utilize these practices right away. The grounding exercises become a deep internal reservoir to draw from in times of need. Movement is innate in all of us, no matter how able bodied or compromised our bodies are. We have an inherent access to the healing power of movement. The more you and your client practice this relationship with your moving bodies, the more you will strengthen.

Trauma-Informed and Movement-Sensitive Therapy

"Seeing trauma as an internal dynamic grants us much-needed agency."

—Gabor Maté, *The Myth of Normal*

We tend to think of trauma as the event that happened to us. Clients come to our practice because they want to rid themselves of the symptoms and stories of high-stress and traumatic events. The suffering that comes from the impact of trauma has many facets, but mostly a sense of disconnection from our body and the safety within ourselves in relation to the external world. What is shattered with trauma is a sense of belonging, connection, trust, and safety.

When my clients come for trauma healing, I don't start by asking what happened or why. I start by asking and listening for *how* these events have shaped them within. *How has the attachment trauma made you feel abandoned and not trusting of human connections? How has that loss of a loved one disconnected you from feeling hopeful? How has the war experience cut you off from your own livelihood? How have you been shaped in your body by fear or shame?* Answering *how* inspires your client's inquiry and awareness. This curiosity is needed to feel and sense the shaping of trauma in their body. When we don't trust, when we disconnect, when we do not feel, or when we are frightened, we are limiting our moving body into not feeling, not expressing, or not exploring. Over time this limitation becomes a way of being—a *trauma beingness*—that resides in the body.

Being trauma-informed means we as therapists understand the psychobiological responses of the nervous system being activated in response to traumatic experiences. It also means we understand how fight, flight, freeze, and fawn responses are expressed in the body.

As clinicians, we can offer our trauma-informed lens and look for opportunities to help our clients connect with this ancient and deep knowledge of how to move beyond the trauma impact back into a relationship with their body.

Because movement is innate in us, we can utilize this direct pathway into the nervous system to help the client settle their dysregulated nervous system, learn to express feelings and sensations, learn to engage with their rich inner landscape. By connecting with the ventral vagal capacity to feel their body in safe relationship, they can engage with others. When they are feeling safe and connected, they can be open to exploring their limiting belief systems in a new way. When they move their body, they begin to process stress responses and regulate their emotional states.

Moving the body means moving one's perceptions along—nothing is static, nothing lasts. When clients begin to engage with their inner knowing of how to work with the stuck, held, or frightened places in the body, their body will change. The trauma-informed lens is understanding that this work needs to be in the right pacing and timing that suits the client, and in alignment with their unfolding process. The movement tools in this book are invitations to explore and always need to be offered in the mindset of collaboration, curiosity, and alignment with the inner pacing of the client. Movements can be large and expressive or tiny and barely visible on the outside. Bodies that are not able to move much, due to not being able bodied or due to pain, still have the option to feel deep intrinsic movements. Movement is about range and depth of connection, not limited to ability.

The use of movement interventions with trauma clients can help them to:

- Ground emotional anxiety into gentle release movements

- Regulate systemic trauma activation into self-regulated states

- Express a stuck feeling through expressive liberation

- Metabolize high charges in the body into settling and soothing

- Play to engage the body in joyful expressions

- Connect with intrinsic motions for inner knowledge

- Feel movement as a social connection with others

When we are movement sensitive, we look for the actual movements of the body that are there and imagine the movements that could be happening but are not yet embodied. We are inviting the client to engage with their moving body to discover what is needed and wanted—for example, noticing a tremor in the body, sensing it, and acknowledging the shaking that is happening. Next is often where therapists fall short: knowing how to facilitate working through that movement and offer options on how to work with it. For example, we can offer to invite movement qualities, pace, or textures. That's why this book is here, to help you skillfully use movement as a diagnostic and therapeutic tool.

Think of a painting and the negative space where the artist has not painted the canvas yet. This possibility of potential colors and shapes that can be imagined is akin to what the client can discover through movement. Trauma limits and cuts off emotions, imagination, creativity, and flow, whereas movement connects and heals what can't be named or verbalized easily.

Trauma-sensitive movement is needed when we want to intervene with the moving body in mind. We can learn about the movement expression of the client by paying attention to how they move and what is being communicated on a deeper and unconscious level. And we can learn to unlock the limiting movement patterns that can keep our clients stuck for a long time.

Notice how clients shift their postures, such as sitting with clenched shoulders as they are recounting a grief memory. Pay attention when there are facial tics or nervous knees bouncing as an expression of anxiety. Track for eye movements that are unusual, perhaps that are nervously scanning the environment for safety. Track how the client walks into the room, how the body moves excitedly to greet you or not. We can learn the silent movement repertoire of our clients to understand their inner world in a more accurate and attuned way than if we focus only on the pure content of their narrative.

Another facet of movement sensitivity is being aware of your own impulses and movements in response to the material or the client's movements. This somatic countertransference is natural as we move with others in resonance. Trauma work—and being movement sensitive—isn't just about the client but about the therapist and the client in relation to each other. Both are breathing, sensing, feeling, and moving together. I like to say that therapy is actually a dialogue of movement. It's a dance.

We start to empathically mirror clients without thinking about it. This leads to being in somatic resonance. It can be a tool for attunement but also trigger our own sensory memories that we must deal with. Part of the work then—and what some of the tools in this book offer—is to wisely work through our own movements both outside and inside the therapy room.

Shifting Perceptions, Identity, and Self-Awareness

"Move your body and your mind will calm."
—Manuela Mischke-Reeds

Your client's body awareness is a crucial ally. When we work with movement in the therapeutic process, we want to shift internal references of perception. Shifting perceptions through movement allows the client to see how they have become identified with their trauma narrative. Feelings of depression or anxiety can influence the perceptions that movement is not possible.

In the beginning, movement is often met with resistance; the mind wants to overpower and say "I don't want to. What good will this do?" But once the body moves, the innate wisdom arises. At first the client might feel stiff, collapsed, or awkward, not knowing how to move. There can be feelings of shame and hurt—all movements away from feeling grounded, liberated, and open—and these begin to impact both mental and physical health.

When movement is introduced and the client accepts that invitation, very quickly the body begins to metabolize the held-back feelings inside it. You might see a relaxation response such as yawning or a kind of cat-stretching, and a sense of somatic release in the body arises. The previous hypervigilance and anxiety calm down. With the shifted somatic state, the mind begins to relax and ease. New present-moment perceptions open up; new experiences and thoughts arise. What was previously seen or felt as threatening is now okay, safe, or neutral. It is not uncommon for my clients to say, "Now that I have moved my body, I feel better, and what I thought 20 minutes ago doesn't seem so intense or relevant anymore." With movement, the mind shifts as the body calms.

I often say to my clients that when they move their body with intention and mindfulness, the mind follows, inviting release and regulated calm. When we offer movement as an intervention, our clients' psychobiology responds. Just as the body responds to threat through moving in fight, flight, freeze, or fawn, the intentional therapeutic movements reduce trauma triggers and emotional reactivity. With greater body awareness, perceptions shift—all of which leads to more clarity of mind and being present with what truly needs attention.

Most trauma experiences are coupled with avoidance or protective behavior and fear, understandably so, but when we are teaching our clients to embody through movement, we are connecting them back with their inner healing capacity to be with the challenges of their lives. When the client's body gets less activated, the feeling of safety comes forth naturally. In these moments, their fear ceases in the brain and the interoceptive capacities are regulated, meaning that they can sense and be with their body's feelings in emotional safety. In short, the capacity of being with the trauma memories, feelings, and sensations can be now examined and processed. It increases the client's ability to deal with negative feelings and challenging memories.

Once clients learn to trust movement as a tool for healing, they are able to reap the benefits of mental clarity, see their patterns of behavior, and lift the shame and stuckness that "bad" body feelings can entrap. This is a powerful shift that can be accomplished in a very short time.

Seven Reasons to Bring Movement into Therapy

Before we launch into the first bundle of exercises, which are designed for therapists, let's quickly review the top reasons that movement should be part of your trauma-informed approach:

1. You bring variation to your therapy work.

2. You offer deeper somatic trauma-resolution techniques.

3. Clients who are kinesthetic will feel met and valued.

4. The work is more effective because you expand on your relational interventions.

5. It's diagnostic. You can literally read the moving body to identify where there is stuck, unprocessed trauma.

6. You learn to track a moving body telling unspoken stories that offer clues as to how the client interacts in the world and how they perceive themselves, others, and their past.

7. Movement makes us more empathic. Our mirror neurons begin firing when we see movement, and by being with movement we better understand the client's inner world, which sometimes holds unexplainable, unspeakable horrors. Movement is a direct line of communication to these events—and to healing.

Rethinking Movement in Psychotherapy

PURPOSE

This worksheet prepares you to rethink the use of movement. Most therapists do not receive any training in movement interventions or even how to perceive the movement of the client. Therefore, when we think of movement in psychotherapy, we might think the following:

- The client moves around to get comfortable.

- The client moves their body to discharge their stress.

- The client expresses a movement through gestures and posture.

Rarely do we think that:

- Movement is a diagnostic tool.

- Movement is an expression of a deeper underlying feeling.

- Movement is a way to directly work somatically.

- Movement is a relational tool in therapeutic work.

- Movement is an intervention for trauma responses to be processed.

- Movement is a tool for self-regulation.

INSTRUCTIONS

Let's examine how you think and feel about the use of movement in psychotherapy. Write down your responses to the following prompts.

When you think of the use of movement in psychotherapy, what images or words come to mind?

_____

_____

_____

When you think of the client's need to move, how do you feel? Check the box that best matches your response:

- ❑ Unsure and inclined to ignore the client's movement

- ❑ Unsure and inclined to encourage or allow their movement

- ❑ Not interested that the client is moving

❑ Comfortable with their moving but not sure what to do with it

❑ Comfortable with their moving and curious to engage with it

❑ Comfortable with their moving as a diagnostic tool

How do you view movement? Is movement to you a behavior, feeling, sensation, cultural expression, or functional necessity?

_____

_____

_____

Now, make a mental shift and entertain the view that the movement of the client is a deep expression of their unique composition of how they feel, process, sense, think, and express. Think of a client who moves in session and you don't quite know what to make of that movement. Shift your perspective; view their movement as an expression of a deeper world within. What is that movement quality that you perceive? What is that saying to you? What are you learning about the client now as you see them as movement?

Write down your impressions of the client through the movement lens. What more do you perceive now that you have shifted your perspective?

_____

_____

_____

_____

_____

_____

_____

_____

_____

_____

Moving Without a Script

PURPOSE

This is a movement exercise that will get you familiar with movement as a therapeutic tool *for yourself*. It's a mindful exploration of your movement and its impact on your nervous system and process. It can help you notice any inner roadblocks and learn to invite your moving body with kindness and safety. If movement is comfortable for you, you can also use this tool to check in with yourself and take a temperature read on your own process (you can skip to step 3 in this case). If it helps, you can play some music in the background, as a support. Avoid dancing "to" the music—allow the music to support your expression.

INSTRUCTIONS

1. Contemplate what arises for you when you read the following lines:

   • My body is allowed to move freely.

   • I am graceful and fluid.

   • Movement is who I am.

   • It's okay to express my moving self.

   Notice what comes up for you. Do any images or narratives come up? What about any negative inner narratives? Can you accept the affirming statements?

2. Write down the internal narratives or statements that came up. How are they impacting your expression right now? What is the inner script of your moving body? Is there an inner voice that says you *can't*, *won't*, or *shouldn't* be or act a certain way? Write it down and with that release any voice of dissent.

   _____

   _____

   _____

   _____

   _____

   _____

   _____

3. Next, set a timer for a minimum of 5 minutes, ideally 15 minutes. Stand and feel your feet on the ground. Ask a simple question into your body: What movement wants to happen right now? Let yourself move in any way that feels just right to you. Notice if you can follow your body expression without any script. Then rest and listen into your body. What is the inner narrative now?

_____

_____

_____

_____

_____

_____

_____

4. Notice any resistance that comes up and see if you can gently inquire what is here. What is the movement of the resistance?

_____

_____

_____

_____

_____

_____

_____

Movement Diary

PURPOSE

Use this tool to learn about your own movement exploration and the personal themes that come up in the practices. Because movement practices can bring up surprising experiences that you may not immediately understand, it can be helpful to start charting for yourself the arc of your process. Movement is nonlinear and we need time to see and feel our way through the moving process. Otherwise, we can lose track of the deeper themes that are actually coming to the foreground. This is the "silent realm" in which movement expresses what words can't. The diary is about your personal experience and will help you to be a more grounded and resilient therapist in service of the client's process.

INSTRUCTIONS

You can use this diary daily or find another rhythm that works for you. I suggest using this diary when you are working on a theme within yourself that is stuck or needs focus or clarity. Another way to use this diary is in relation to your client's work. You can note what comes up in therapeutic work and then use the movement practices to somatically resource your nervous system. These are all helpful ways to keep track of your own countertransference and become more effective in your work.

For each diary entry, note the following:

- **Date/Time:** Record the date and time.

- **Practice/Exercise:** Note which practice you are exploring.

- **My Personal Themes:** What stories or memories are coming up?

- **Movement Process:** What felt new, exciting, or familiar? What other qualities do you notice?

- **Body Awareness:** What are your body feelings now?

- **Reflection:** Write what comes up after the practice.

- **Countertransference:** What got triggered with your client?

Date/Time	Practice/Exercise	My Personal Themes	Movement Process	Body Awareness	Reflection	Countertransference

CHAPTER 2

CONSIDERATIONS WHEN WORKING WITH MOVEMENT

"When one settled body encounters another, there can be a deeper settling of both bodies. But when one unsettled body encounters another, the unsettling tends to compound in both bodies."

—**Resmaa Menakem,** *My Grandmother's Hands*

Bringing movement into sessions is not without a few barriers. The biggest challenge is not knowing how to do it; every tool and exercise in this book will help with that. Another large hurdle is not having fluency when transitioning from the talking to the moving; chapters 3, 4, and 5 offer ways to build your confidence so that this barrier doesn't prevent you from making progress with a client. In this chapter, we will look at the following additional considerations: bodies of oppression, cultural competency, shame and stigma, and mobility.

The Oppressed Body in Movement

"If you put your psyche in motion it will heal itself."

—**Gabrielle Roth,** *Maps to Ecstasy*

The moving body is the whole body. We move in relation to the totality of who we are. Movement is an expression or sense of our body stories, as they explore deeply who we are in relation to all our embodied experiences. When we work with the moving body we are working with living stories from the past to the present. We are inviting the client to experience the complexity of their historical relationship with self and others. The somatic imprints of systems of oppression are often felt in the body not as conscious thought.

Oppression patterns can be experienced in the family, community, society, culture, institutions, religious schooling, political system, and more. Trauma is held in the body through nervous system responses. Fear in a family will be modeled and reinforced through culture, behaviors, and unspoken agreements. These felt experiences are recorded in the body's cellular memory often at a young age; we don't realize this until we begin to wake up in our bodies. Our felt sense of ancestral connections, historical trauma, or collective trauma often is revealed with movement, as we tap into the unspoken shapes and feelings that were imprinted and held in response to an oppressed situation. Until we become consciously aware and begin moving with that unspoken realm, we often don't realize these patterns of oppression.

Bring to your work a view of how the client has learned to see themselves through the lens of others and how this has impacted their inner freedom to express and move. That will give you a clue as to how these unconscious patterns have shown up in their body. As somatic movement therapists, we need to be inclusive of the embodied experiences shaped by gender, race, culture, sexual identity and orientation, class, ideas, ageism, ancestors, cultural body perceptions, and projections. When we work with trauma our somatic movement interventions need to be understood in the context of how our clients have been experiencing body oppression in their culture of origin and the dominant culture currently. We can't ignore or separate the complexity of what it means to be embodied from the client's experience of oppression.

When my torture-survivor clients from Southeast Asia and Central America testified in court to prove they had grounds for refugee status, they were not believed. Their severe sexual trauma left them stifled, frozen in their terror—and not behaving in the ways that were expected of a victim. Cultural insensitivity and language barriers added to their dismissal. Their already traumatized bodies were then re-traumatized when they were told that they were making up their stories. Being dismissed was a reminder of how the impulse to be free and move—literally and metaphorically—was once again overpowered.

In therapy, we need to have this in mind, as we are always moving with the body in relation to the person's complex relationship with their culture and systems of oppression. In my clients, the body of incarceration and torture was a distinct experience that was triggered every time they had to go to court or answer to authorities. This *somatic social location* (a concept we will explore further in chapter 6) induced body postures, gestures, and behaviors of survival, as well as trauma memories that were reinforced with each trauma-insensitive encounter.

When these bodies showed up in the therapy room, the invitation to move and explore triggered all kinds of associated memories of oppression. Therefore, *how* we invite our clients into movement healing is critical. This includes being sensitive to the oppressed body and being compassionate when we are inviting the moving experience. Rushing, impatience, agendas, goals, or even the expectation that movement is wonderful is not helpful.

We as therapists need to understand our own stories of body oppression and be consciously curious about theirs. (The exercise *Self-Reflection on Body Oppression* is a good start.) The qualities that come to mind here are: warm, slow, inviting, curious, gentle, kind, playful, respectful, compassionate, understanding, infinitely patient, emotionally attuned, offering gentle advocacy, being okay with discomfort, and caring. When we embody these qualities, a synchronistic attunement begins to materialize, from soma to soma. The oppressed body recognizes authenticity, genuine care, and compassion, and it seeks healing, resolution, and support. Our work is to find the pathway toward the safe inner experience.

Cultural and Diversity Awareness

"Boundaries are the distance at which I can love you and me simultaneously."

—Prentis Hemphill, *What It Takes to Heal*

Movement is universal. All cultures have practices of movement. But the sensitivities around when and how and with whom to move vary greatly.

It is important for a trauma-informed therapist to be sensitive to how movement is received and perceived. For some clients, movement is necessary for their bodies and they are very comfortable with it and seek that kind of work. For others, movement is unacknowledged or expressed privately.

Gauge the client's comfort level by asking them and by informing them that movement can be part of the therapeutic work in many different ways. Movement can be done in the chair very quietly and intrinsically or it can be done very expressively and expansively, using the whole room. All of them are valid explorations if they serve the client.

Movement heightens body awareness and, with that, potential shame around body image. Being receptive and sensitive to these themes coming up is core to working with movement. You can gently bring the topic of body shame into movement in a powerful way that often can't be expressed in words. Always respect the *no*—if the client does not want to move or feels self-conscious about what you name and see, gently and kindly bring that awareness in and let it go for another time.

Avoid making assumptions about your clients or their movements based on their identity or culture. Watch out for your own biases and stereotypes around movement; there are many. Spend some time looking at this within yourself and examine it. The more awareness you have around this topic, the more you can sensitively offer movement explorations that are healing and free from assumptions.

Removing the Stigma of the Moving Body

"Dance is communication and thus fulfills a basic human need."

—Marian Chace

One of the negative ingrained cultural belief systems around the moving body is the notion that only certain bodies can or should move. Clients commonly express, "I can't move—I am not a dancer," "I feel ashamed of moving my body," "I'm embarrassed about how I will look and what others will think," "I feel awkward." Working with such beliefs will be an essential part of the therapeutic focus as you introduce the tools in this book. You will need to listen carefully for this internalized belief that stifles the motivation or courage to move.

In much of Western culture we are not taught to see movement as a therapeutic tool. When we do, movement interventions are often considered a kind of dancing. Dancing is a subset of movement; it can be expressive, creative, fun, subtle, and an art form. Movement in the therapeutic context has a more specific focus that is not concerned with performance. The client uses movement to express their inner world and access what they have not been able to verbalize.

There is a long history of dance/movement therapy (DMT) through the incredible work of pioneers such as Marian Chace, Trudi Schoop, Liljan Espenak, Mary Starks Whitehouse, Joan Chodorow, and Janet Adler. They recognized the healing power of dance and movement techniques, using them with a variety of patients that were challenging to reach emotionally. These pioneers understood the moving body as a direct and silent expression of what was lying inside wanting to be seen. They also engaged in the nonverbal dialogue of *mirroring*: dancing with the client to help them to come into a relationship with the symbolic language of sensations, through which their longing, fears, anxiety, and anger could be safely expressed.

We sometimes forget that we're tribal creatures, that we have moved and danced in community throughout our existence. Moving together is as ancient as humanity. We know that moving in dyads or as a group has tremendous co-regulating capacities. When we move together, no matter our spoken language, we come into a deeper understanding, a more essential human dialogue. We hear, feel, and sense each other through our bodies and learn of the interior world of the other. This transcends our differences and brings forth connections we couldn't imagine prior to the moving experience.

It's important for therapists to learn how to facilitate, mirror, and join in movement. For the client new to movement, we start small, in the chair, with motions of the hands, neck, or other places in the body that are easily accessible. Movement is already there, expressed through a fist, a clenched jaw, a repeated motion of the shoulder, a jiggling leg, a shuffling foot—our job is to notice and gently invite the body into self-exploration thought movement. The exercise *Using Language the Body Can Hear* is an ideal first step.

People with Limited Movement Ability

"Movement is life."

—Moshe Feldenkrais, *Awareness Through Movement*

This book assumes a degree of ability in the body to move. Each body is different, and each body's story is different. Yet every body is able to move to a certain degree; sometimes it means the breath is the principal mover. As you suggest these exercises, please be sensitive to the limitations that bodies can have. You might need to adjust practices to make them workable for your client. The externally visible movement may be small and intrinsic, yet the benefit within can be enormous. Read through the instructions for the exercise first and make sure your client can do those steps. If not, you can always modify them.

Clients tend to make assumptions about their body's limitations that are based on their fears. When working with your client, be aware of their window of tolerance in relation to their ability. For example, an injury in the shoulder may limit their *ability* to raise their arm over their head, while their *window of tolerance* may limit their movement to just shoulder height. There is still space between the two points that can be explored, as long as you are respectful and sensitive to the client's fear of movement. Notice when they might be holding back a movement because they are afraid of the limitations arising or are experiencing a feeling of shame coming up. Work with them on shifting their thought from "This can't be done" to "How can I make this accessible now?" This change in mindset helps them to focus not on what the body is unable to do, but what the body *is* able to participate in right now. Rather than the exploration getting cut short, it is engaged with positively.

Approach clients' limitations with attention and care. Be creative, and invite small and doable steps. You can begin with the tool *The Able Zone of Tolerance*. Chapter 13, which explores breath, sound, and intrinsic movement, can also be very helpful when working with clients who have a limited range of motion or limited ability. Accommodate the client's needs, such as inviting them to move in the chair rather than on the floor. Listen carefully to what the client needs and offer suggestions to make the experience successful for them. A sensation of well-being, the joy of feeling connected to oneself deeply, the release of a stuck trauma pattern moving through the body—these are all important signs of healing.

Considerations When Working with Physical Pain

"There is that in us which has moved from the very beginning:
it is that which can liberate us."

—Mary Starks Whitehouse, *"The Tao of the Body"*

Managing pain is both uncomfortable and exhausting. All our protective mechanisms are activated when we are navigating the pained body. Often that means moving less, restricting the range of motion, or becoming both physically and emotionally frozen. Moreover, the secondary emotional responses of frustration, anger, irritation, grief, and rejection are very close. In short, the last thing we wish to do is move our body and feel the pain.

Yet there are qualities of "emotional movement" that we can invite our clients who are experiencing physical pain to explore. Connecting with the moving body is part of igniting the innate healing capacity. The vulnerable body brings forth the soft and tender parts within that need healing and support. Moving with pain is a deep conversation with the body's limits, hurts of the past, scars from trauma, and invasive procedures endured. These markers of trauma on the client's body are part of their living history—and they can be brought into healing.

One of my clients had suffered debilitating trauma from severe physical torture. Her body had nerve damage and touch was excruciating, and yet so yearned for. Movements that were beyond maintaining her body's function were perceived as a threat and a reminder that the trauma memories could resurface. The range of motion in her shoulders was restricted, her hips felt stiff, and she did not feel comfortable on the floor. She perceived her body as a prison to be endured and not enjoyed, stating, "I feel like a brittle, broken paper doll."

Working with a somatic psychotherapist was a big challenge for her, and she felt ambivalence. Resistance to feeling her brittle and broken body was mixed with deep longing for some physical relief and the aliveness she imagined she had lost. Big movements set off a mild panic as she immediately felt incapable of doing anything and was met with a wall of searing pain in various places in her body. But she was able to engage with these movements by practicing the *Befriending the Pained Body* exercise and beginning the process of inviting the body as movement. When the reference shifts from *doing* movement to *being* movement, the client is able to enter the experience of their body as it is. New possibilities open up somatically, and the struggle to contain or manage pain can ease.

Self-Reflection on Body Oppression

PURPOSE

This is a writing and reflection inquiry to learn about your own embodied stories of oppression. It can also be used as an ongoing tool as you work with clients who become aware of their internalized oppression. It is helpful to track your own triggers and inspirations as your clients uncover their deeper layers. Let that be an invitation to work on your body stories that go beyond the familiar narratives. Gently and kindly work on this and learn from your own moving soma.

INSTRUCTIONS

1. Sit quietly and ground yourself.

2. Ask your soma for cooperation in this process. For example: "I am opening my body wisdom to this process."

3. Reflect on the common body stories you are familiar with in your life. Notice the familiar places in your body that respond to these stories. For example: "Where and how did I experience moments of oppression? How did my body respond in that moment?"

4. Next, invite inquiry with the following open questions:

   • "Where does the impact of oppression live inside my body?"

   • "How is that place feeling right now?"

   • "What do I need to know about this body place at this moment?"

5. Sit with it . . . let your soma notice . . . be open . . . just notice. If there is a movement, let it simply be.

6. Place a hand on the area of the body you are working with. Take intentional breaths and make contact with that area.

7. Remember that you can pause, stop, and self-regulate at any time. This is a kind inquiry; be open and curious to learn and sense the patterns of oppression so you can recognize them. It is not a marathon or a trigger into trauma material.

8. Take another breath. Notice the absence of movement or the impulse of movement. What are you sensing? What are you feeling? What is the body story right here, right now?

9. Take 15 minutes and journal. Write whatever comes to mind, with no pauses—just write.

TIPS

- Remember this is an ongoing story that is unfolding. You can keep a journal and continue this inquiry over time. It's quite a profound process to see clients healing their body oppressions and notice parallels in your own soma-psyche over time.

- To expand this practice, do the *Write and Move It!* exercise in chapter 8, practicing it for yourself.

Using Language the Body Can Hear

PURPOSE

When we invite the moving body, we need to be mindful of the kind of language we use. The internal noise is often very loud, meaning the client already has lots of self-critical or shaming messages about the body, sensations, and movement. Culturally we have a mindset that often instructs the body to *do* rather than *be*. There is an inherent mind-over-body imprint that can get in the way when we want to learn about the subtleties and inner landscape of the body. The language of the body is different from the thinking or speaking voice. The body responds to kindness and inclusion and unconditional acceptance. Right, wrong, good, and bad are all categories of judgment that have no place in this work.

TIPS

Avoid being a cheerleader; your authentic caring intent and kind voice is what the client needs. Instructions into the body are like gentle letters to the soul. Ideally, you want the client to be able to speak to their own body in this manner; as you facilitate movement, be aware that the language you're using is teaching them how to communicate with their own body. You can encourage them, once they have some practice, to adopt the same language when tuning into their body.

INSTRUCTIONS

1. When you guide a client into their body, make sure you are in your own body connection. Use your breath and sensations to ground and open your sensory perceptions. Receive the client from your soma perception.

2. Pay attention to your tone of voice, cadence, and the kind of instructive words you use.

3. Adopt an invitational attitude with the following qualities:

   - Kindness

   - Being welcoming

   - Inquiring with curiosity

   - Accepting the client's experience no matter what it is

   - Delighting in the experimentation and courage the client shows

4. Use invitational language such as:

   - "See if . . ."

- "Allow yourself . . ."
- "I invite you to . . ."
- "Notice how . . ."
- "As you notice . . ."
- "What else . . ."
- "Now that you _____, see if . . ."
- "Let's inquire . . ."

5. When you are ready to facilitate the movement exercises, begin with the following phrases:

- "See if it feels right to move/breathe/sense in this way . . ."
- "Where do you feel this movement?"
- "What kind of movement are you noticing right now?"
- "What else do you notice as you move your [*arms, legs, etc.*]?"
- "Where does this movement want to go next?"
- "See if this motion has another expression that wants to emerge."
- "How does this movement connect with . . . ?"
- "As you move right now, what else are you aware of?"
- "Notice if there are other parts of your body that want to join this motion."
- "Go ahead and follow that movement."
- "Allow this motion to go all the way to its completion."
- "Now that you relate to this breath, notice the kinds of sensations that come along."
- "Let's inquire into how you experienced . . ."

The Able Zone of Tolerance

PURPOSE

In this exercise, you will explore your range of ability to discover what's possible when using movement. You'll also look at the movements you prefer to do and those you tend to avoid.

INSTRUCTIONS

Fill out this form and share it with your therapist so they know your preferences.

1. What kinds of movement do you prefer? For example, what movements give you joy, make you feel more connected, or bring about positivity?

   _____

   _____

   _____

2. Next, reflect on movements that you can do but avoid, perhaps because you are afraid, or feel shame, or feel a physical or emotional avoidance. You don't have to explain why. Just write down the movements here.

   _____

   _____

   _____

3. Fill in the blanks: "When I write down the movements I can do but avoid, I feel _____

   _____ and my body is _____

   _____."

4. What would you need in order to safely explore those movements? _____

   _____

   _____

5. Use the space below to write or draw what you are discovering about your body in this process.

Befriending the Pained Body

PURPOSE

Movement can be enjoyed by every body, even the body in pain, when there is sufficient understanding and somatic attunement to the client's experience. Learning to listen to the client's body will show a pathway. You just have to be patient and open to seeing it. This exercise introduces three qualities that can change your client's relationship to their body in a positive way.

INSTRUCTIONS

Practice patience and inclusivity of all kinds of body experiences as you invite your client into these reflections. You want to open the possibility for them to engage with movement on their terms, guided by what their body allows. That is often about timing and listening to the body.

Your goal is to support your client in strengthening the following qualities:

- **Self-kindness** for managing the pain and discomfort: *I bring kindness to my body*.
- **Self-compassion** for working on the emotional edges and origins of this pain: *I bring an open heart to my pain*.
- **Self-acceptance** for being in this body at this time: *I make space for this body as it is*.

REFLECTION

Discuss these questions with your client before and after the movement exploration:

- Where in my body do I feel pain or compromise?
- What parts of my body are wanting help to protect me or manage this pain?
- What areas in my body are neutral or feel good, or am I able to approach with open curiosity?
- What can I do and what can't I do right now?
- How can I make room for this body to move, even in the smallest of ways?
- What movement feels like an ally on my healing path?

CHAPTER 3

PREPARING YOURSELF AND YOUR SPACE

"When therapeutic agreements are clear and a therapeutic alliance feels trustworthy, the client can risk inner explorations."

—**Kylea Taylor,** *The Ethics of Caring*

Therapeutic movement work involves exploring body postures in space, as well as a different relationship to how we use the usual therapy space. There are four main components to bringing movement into your work:

1. Physical space

2. Therapeutic mindset

3. Moving with or witnessing

4. Language the body experiences

Let's look at each component in more detail; the exercises in this chapter will help you to explore this aspect further. In addition, the education piece of this chapter ends with a list of tips for what to do and not do when getting ready for movement therapy.

Physical Space

Designating a space for movement ahead of time will help you maintain professional boundaries and continue the therapeutic safety you establish with your client. You want these transitions not to be an obstacle but to support your work. The physical distance might shift, so be aware of what that does to your therapeutic relationship. It can be very powerful and enhance the work, especially when you bring this in consciously.

You do not need a dance studio; small spaces can work just fine. Just make sure your space is inviting and accommodating, so that you can transition easily into movement work. You want to have it set up so that you can easily move back and forth from sitting to moving. Avoid moving furniture around with the client there; movement work will feel like an afterthought to the client if the room isn't already prepared. Make sure there is enough space for yourself and the client. A floor chair or a meditation pillow is helpful.

You want clients to be comfortable when they are standing, lying down, sitting on the floor, or moving around the space a bit.

Doing floor work invites many possibilities that are potentially new to the client. Being on the floor can bring forth playfulness, a sense of comfort in the body, and ease from not having to "sit up straight" on the therapy couch. Often this brings a somatic shift in perception simply by moving to the floor. Some clients find being on the ground less formal. That means more potential therapeutic closeness, which will mean you have to reestablish your therapeutic boundaries. Design the transition to and from the floor with that in mind. Make sure you can shift to all the levels in your office—whether standing with the client, sitting in a chair, or sitting on the floor—with ease, without feeling the therapeutic container is getting wobbly or unsafe.

Some clients might find this arrangement unfamiliar and not know how to be without the traditional chair-to-chair therapy setting. You can model the transition and how to do this by practicing standing with them.

Clients sometimes like to roll around and get into sensing their bodies; it's often a great entryway into this work. If they want to stay on the floor, talking while they are stretching, this is good. Some clients can't transition to the floor, so make sure you can adapt the exercises to their body's ability. Some clients might want to do floor work but need help or extra pillows and support. Plan so that all clients, even those with compromised bodies, feel welcome.

Finally, consider what it is like to move in that spot and try it out. If you feel safe and comfortable, the client likely will too. In fact, make this space where you resource yourself through movement! In between sessions, it can be very helpful to lie down and ground yourself, release tension, and resource your moving body. See the therapist exercise *Movement-Friendly Office Space Checklist* for more tips.

Therapeutic Mindset

"The core of the movement experience is the sensation of moving and being moved."

—Mary Starks Whitehouse, "The Tao of the Body"

Your therapeutic mindset matters when you bring in movement. See if you can adopt a curious, dynamic, and open attitude. Movement in its very nature is dynamic and ever-shifting; the discovery process and the impact on the body's nervous system and overall well-being are all part of it.

Adopting the following qualities will allow you to help clients with self-discovery:

- Openness to the outcome

- Curiosity about the process that emerges

- Kindness toward any self-critical inner voices or shame

- Encouragement when things get tough

- Compassionate presence when trauma's pain shows up in the body

- Presence when the change comes forth

- Listening when new meanings are revealed

Movement explorations are not static, so learning to "flow" with the changes will be important. Be open and receptive to your client's journey. Like any protocol that is experiential, it is an invitation and the beginning of a dialogue. You want to avoid reading a script but rather guide the client through the exercises. Every tool has a purpose or intention, and yet it's the client who will make it meaningful; help them to drop in and find their own way with it.

In addition, the more comfortable you are with moving in your body and using movement as a therapeutic tool, the more comfortable the client will be. Make sure you have tried the tools first so you are familiar with them in your own body.

The tool *Movement Diary* in chapter 1 can help you track the moving "weather patterns" in your own body.

Movement is a powerful gateway into unconscious material beliefs and feelings. You want to be prepared for that and ground your own body in the moving space. Because movement work can express, affect, and change a lot, you will need to learn to regulate yourself in this dynamic situation. Doing the exercises in this chapter will help a great deal with regulating your own nervous system. Use your breath to calm and your somatic markers to anchor your own experience in relationship to the moving client. See the exercise *Somatic Anchor and Grounding Breath* for one regulating technique.

Moving With or Witnessing

"The witness's experience is completely dependent on the presence of the mover, who is the primary catalyst for all that stirs within her. The mover's experience is completely dependent on the presence of the witness."

—**Janet Adler,** *Offering from the Conscious Body*

A big question arises when you do floor and movement work: *Should I move with the client or not?* It depends on both the comfort level of the client and your intentions for the exercise.

Humans are used to moving in space together; we are wired to move in dyads or as a group as a way to establish connection, safety, and belonging. We know from research on mirror neurons that when we see another person's movement, the same neuronal connection fires in our own body (Shafir, 2016). That brings forth empathy, comfort, and the sense of "I am not alone," which can be very beneficial if the client feels shy, is working on connection, or needs encouragement to try something new.

Conversely, it can feel alienating to a client when you invite them to move but stay seated in your chair as if you are observing them. This can bring forth shame, a sense of being exposed, or a feeling of being scrutinized under a magnifying glass and needing to perform and do it right. You want to remove these obstacles by framing the exploration and also offering your participation. You can suggest that the movement the client is exploring can be mirrored by you and done together. For many clients that is a comfort. When the client is not feeling self-conscious, mirroring can be supportive and encouraging.

If the exploration involves you moving with the client, then you can bring some attention to the different physical distances by saying: "Notice how this feels to you. I am standing closer to you. As I move with you here, what do you notice?" Bring the attention back to the client's experience. If you are sitting on the floor, you might ask, "How is this for you, that we are both on the ground? Are there any adjustments you want me to make? Is the distance okay?" Then make the adjustments that are comfortable for both you and the client.

If the exploration doesn't involve your participation, you still want to position yourself at the client's level. When the client stands and moves, also move your body to serve as a standing witness and guide. Don't stay seated. Same with the floor: if the client lies down or moves on the floor, sit on the floor as a seated witness.

Here are a few more tips:

- Look out for the physical safety of the client. Make sure when they move that they have room and will not bump into objects within the space.

- Be extra mindful of your boundaries.

- Notice and listen to what wants to happen.

- Relax yourself and enjoy the movement.

- If you are invited to mirror and move with the client, let yourself feel and sense into your body and the movement as well. The more authentic you are, the more encouraged the client will be.

- If you're asked to sit and witness, hold the space and track the story arc of the movement. Tracking is covered in detail in chapter 4.

Language

"Dance is the hidden language of the soul."

—Martha Graham

When a client comes to you for the first time, tell them that your work includes floor work and invite them to view and explore the designated space. Even if they are not interested at first, there might be an opening later when they feel they want to sit or lie down on the floor. You can ask: "How would you like to be in the space? Standing, lying down, sitting?" Give them agency and allow them to get comfortable.

When you see an opportunity for movement work, frame the exercises as explorations that will give the client ownership and let them settle into their way of moving. Use helpful language, such as that described in *Using Language the Body Can Hear* in chapter 2 and *Scripts to Explore Movement* in this chapter.

Think of your voice as a conduit to reach into the client's body through your tone and rhythm. When you speak mindfully and leave pauses, the client can feel their experience and be with what is happening. If they have to think about your guidance it means they are not embodied but rather mediating their movement experience through their mind. You want to pause to leave room for the client to process. Choose your words with care and use language that is inviting. Be mindful of instructional language that can elicit resistance. You want to speak *into* the body and not *at the body*. That means short, kind invitations that are open for the client to interpret in their own way.

The Movement Container

When I consult, therapists will ask me, "Do I need training to teach movement?" Training can be helpful, yes, but it's not mandatory. Having taught movement for decades, I believe you only need two things to add this tool to your repertoire: *curiosity* and *your own body*. You already know how to move. You *are* movement. So play some music, get on the floor, move in nature, listen to your body, and play, play, play.

Let's look briefly at some best practices when doing movement with your client. If you follow these basic ground rules, you can be assured of delivering targeted movement interventions to your clients.

WHAT TO DO

- **Read the instructions** all the way through before working with an exercise.

- **Try the exercise yourself first** with the client in mind. Feel it within your own body with the body ability of your client in mind. Be creative; make adjustments. Consider how the exercise can be more accessible. For example, you might offer a sitting alternative, make the movement just in one area of the body and not the whole body, make the movement smaller or bigger, or change the speed of it.

- **Create an inviting physical space** that includes a place to lie down on a couch rather than the floor. Many clients have a difficult time going up and down from the floor.

- **Introduce movement as an "exploration,"** which means it can be changed at any time. Use invitational language the body hears. You can say, "Let me suggest an exploration . . . how is that for you?" Framing it this way reduces the chance of the client rejecting movement outright.

- **Gently focus the client on the movement they are able to do** and not the types of movement they can't do. Name what can be possible to explore and wait for the client to engage. Have the client lead with their own experience. Make contact with the movement the client is curious about.

- **Be sensitive to feelings** of grief, loss, and pain that arise. Offer encouragement to trust the movement and continue. Also make room for tender feelings, especially body shame. When traumatic material surfaces, stay in contact with the client and encourage them to move through what their body is offering. You can say, "Trust your body right now."

- **Move with the client** if they feel shy or need mirroring to support a relational movement intervention. Also be sensitive to the client's movement needs—adjust and be creative, adapting any tools to the client's needs and level of safety.

- **Take breaks** when overwhelm, confusion, or fear comes up that can't be processed.

- **Keep your verbal instructions clear and concise** so that the client is immersed in their experience.

- **Be mindful of your voice modulation**, how you speak to the client.

- **Ask open-ended questions**, be curious, and let the meaning arise from the client's experience.

- **Allow pauses and reflection time** at the end of the protocols.

WHAT NOT TO DO

Following the previous tips will go a long way. But here are a few standout things to watch out for when bringing in movement to therapy.

- **Don't focus on whether the process will yield results.** Often that has to do with not being patient and not trusting the process of the moving exploration itself. See if you can adopt a positive and curious attitude when guiding your client through these exercises.

- **Don't be too scripted or solutions-focused.** Remember that movement is dynamic and changing, which is a big healing factor. Clients discover, shift, and change, and the expressiveness of a movement is a big part of this work. Stay open to what emerges and allow space for the client to self-discover.

- **Don't interrupt a movement process** that is ongoing. You can track for activation levels in the body and offer resources and grounding when needed. And you can take pauses and ask the client to be with the experience, but try to avoid interrupting it.

- **Don't interpret for the client.** Let them make the meaning of their experience. You can encourage this by asking open-ended questions such as "What do you notice as you feel . . . ?" "How are you experiencing this image right now?" "As you sense into this motion, what is that communicating to you right now?"

- **Don't dismiss movement tools** as purely expressive. Treat them as valid therapeutic interventions. Where does the movement lead within? What is behind this moving experience? Clients will minimize their own experience if you don't hold the value that this is a depth process to be accessed.

TELEHEALTH TIPS

Clients can feel awkward or self-conscious when moving in front of a camera. It can bring up issues of being watched or judged. Body image issues or shame can arise. You want to make the movement experience safe and comfortable for the client when they are meeting with you virtually. In addition to the general tips for introducing movement, keep these best practices in mind during an online session:

- **Name the telehealth limitations** and suggest options. For example, it's okay for the client to turn their camera off or move out of the frame so as not to be visible.

- **Create safety and a sense of self-agency** for the client. Allow them to choose how they want to set this up: "How would you like to move? You can stay in the frame or move out of it and explore this motion without me seeing it." Over time it is likely that they will want to share their movement with you. The main goal is their emotional safety and comfort.

- **Ensure they have space to move.** Ask if their space is safe and appropriate for movement activities. Ask them to look around and make sure they have room to move.

Movement-Friendly Office Space Checklist

If you want to make your space movement-friendly, here is a short checklist of what would be helpful to set up.

☐ **Designate an open space** that is not cluttered, with no furniture obstructing it.

☐ **Have a comfortable clean carpet,** a mat, or a thick blanket ready so that you can invite the client into doing floor work.

☐ **Make sure the space is warm** and keep extra blankets on hand. An extra heater nearby can be helpful. When the client is doing floor work, their body may cool down.

☐ **Offer warm, unobtrusive lighting.**

☐ **Consider privacy.** For example, make sure your client will not feel exposed in front of a window.

☐ **Have on hand items to roll on,** such as bouncy balls, foam rollers, and small tennis balls.

☐ **Have a pillow or floor chair for yourself** that lives in that space. This will also indicate that there is a second therapy space in the room. I keep a second notepad in that area so I don't have to shuffle my notes around.

☐ **Consider the abilities of your client** and make accommodations ahead of time.

☐ **If you are doing telehealth, ensure both spaces are prepped.** Tell your client that you might bring in movement and discuss their needs and setup for their space. Consider your own telehealth setup as well. I have a standing desk that moves up and down, which is very handy. When the client stands on Zoom, I adjust my desk and camera so that the client can see and feel that I am standing and moving with them, and I ask them to adjust their camera so I can see their body if they are comfortable doing so.

Somatic Anchor and Grounding Breath

PURPOSE

This is a quick on-the-go practice while you are guiding movement with your client and want to regulate yourself back into a sense of grounding. This will help you to not get stuck in your own nervous system dysregulation, and you can repeat this throughout the session. This exercise requires practice, so repeat it often.

INSTRUCTIONS

1. Find one or two places in the body you know are anchors for you. For example, when you stand with the client, are your feet in a grounding place? When you sit, is your spine straight and relaxed and are you resting evenly on your sitz bones? Is your belly relaxed? Do you have an open chest?

2. Slowly and quietly exhale, letting the breath out of gently parted lips, while you hold in mind the somatic anchor in your body. That is all. You simply place your attention on the somatic anchor while you slowly exhale. The exhale is not audible to the client; it's like a gentle mist. Think of grounding your breath *into* the somatic anchor in your body.

3. Take one or two more breaths and direct your attention to the anchor places. Notice how there is an instant shift. You can then let go and move on.

4. Since you don't have the time to divert away from your client, you will practice this as a dual awareness practice. When you notice that you are getting ungrounded, remind yourself right away of your somatic anchors and then shift the breath there for 30 seconds.

You might have to repeat this throughout the session. It will eventually come as second nature to you as you work.

List your top five somatic anchors:

1. _____

2. _____

3. _____

4. _____

5. _____

After the session with your client, reflect on how that went. What did you learn? Which somatic anchor in your body works the best? When do you tend to get dysregulated during sessions with your clients? What are the indicators that you are getting dysregulated and are in need of anchoring and grounding?

_____

_____

_____

_____

_____

Scripts to Explore Movement

PURPOSE

Use invitational language that the body can hear. You want to bookend the movement explorations with a mindful entry as well as an ending. That way it feels contained and safe, and the client will want to try this in the future.

TIPS

Of course, movement work can also happen on the chair or the couch. Small gestures, small body movements, and intrinsic motion do not need to be explored on the floor or standing up. Starting in the chair and making the client more aware that movement is not necessarily dancing but sensing small motions and impulses in the body is a safe way to teach the client to trust their moving body to stay seated. Many of the tools in this book are designed so that clients can stay in the chair.

INSTRUCTIONS

1. **Frame the movement/floor work exercise:** Make clear why you are suggesting the exercise at this time. Examples: *I noticed you were doing this movement, and I wonder if you would like to explore that more by moving to the floor? The theme you just discussed—we could bring that into a more physical experience. It seems like your body may want to move and lie down; what do you notice your body telling you? This might support you to deepen your understanding. We can explore this in movement and then we will integrate this talking at the end.*

2. **Get consent:** You can say, *I have a suggestion—we can take this exploration to the floor right now, if you would like to start standing, lying down, or moving around? Would it be okay if you brought this exploration onto the floor and continued that theme? I have some suggestions to guide you through an exploration; would you like to try that?*

3. **Invite mindful movement exploration:** You can suggest, *How about we do an exploration with that? Let's see what your body wants as you do this motion standing, sitting, lying down, or walking. How about you slow down and see what body motion wants to come forth?*

4. **Transition back to sitting:** After the exploration, make sure you leave time to integrate the experience before the client leaves. You want to be as mindful with their exit—getting up from the floor or coming down from standing—as you are with your invitation. For example: *if you're feeling ready, we can move back onto the chairs and continue exploring through words what your body has been exploring through movement. It seems like your body wants to rest and be more still; what do you notice your body saying? Would your body feel more relaxed if we return to the couch to integrate all that we've explored today?*

CHAPTER 4

TRACKING THE MOVING BODY

"The witness practices the art of seeing. Seeing clearly is not about knowing what the mover needs or must do. The witness does not 'look at' the mover, but instead, as she internalizes the mover, she attends to her own experience of judgment, interpretation, and projection and responds to the mover as a catalyst."

—**Janet Adler,** "The Collective Body"

Somatic tracking is a crucial part of the therapy. You'll gain valuable information about your client's baseline, internal experience, comfort level, triggers, patterned responses, regulation, and progress in therapy. With practice, you will excel at noticing small and intrinsic movements, and become adept at engaging with what you are witnessing in the client. Use the exercises in this chapter as guidelines and allow for creativity.

When starting out, it can be somewhat of a challenge to know when to track (and what to track) and when to intervene. The following points will guide you.

WHEN TO TRACK MOVEMENT

- While the client is telling a story, track how the story is being communicated through nonverbal movement.
- When the client is exhibiting trauma-activated hyperarousal or hyperaroused symptoms, read the body movements that are indicating this nervous system arousal (e.g., fidgety movements, flushed skin, more labored or held breath).
- When a client is engaged in functional and transitional movement (e.g., getting in and out of the chair, entering and exiting the room), track how they are moving.

WHAT KINDS OF MOVEMENTS TO TRACK

- Micro-expressions or micro-movements (these often reveal underlying psychological material)
- Spontaneous movement expressions
- Repetitive movements that are connected to the storyline
- Discharging movements that indicate trauma arousal (e.g., tremors and shakes)
- Movements that arise with emotions

WHEN TO INTERVENE

- When a client is activated and needs help to discharge or regulate the emotional charge

- When help is needed to facilitate stuck emotional expression

- When experimenting with new or unfamiliar choices (e.g., setting a boundary)

- When you notice signature movements unique to your client (e.g., a hair flip, repeatedly touching a body part, holding the arm in a particular position)—these repeated movements can offer insight into deeper material

Kinds of Movements

"The symbols of the self arise in the depths of the body."

—Carl Jung

Movement can be divided into the following categories:

- **Functional movement:** Functional actions supporting everyday living—for example, opening the refrigerator, walking across the room, or opening a door.

- **Expressive movement:** Visible movement expressing the underlying narrative, beliefs, emotions, inner state, and so forth unique to a given individual. This includes repetitive gestures and/or postures—for example, self-soothing by rubbing the fingers together.

- **Symbolic movement:** These movements have ritual qualities that express values, myths, or symbols. These can include archetypal movements, such as a prayer position of the hands, that have a personal or collective meaning for the client.

- **Intrinsic movement:** Movement felt inside that's often very subtle and not always visible—for example, movements indicative of a fear state, such as subtle trauma discharge or a deeply held freeze. There can also be subtle positive movements, such as micro-movements in the spine that bring fluidity and openness. Intrinsic movements can be involuntary (e.g., a tremor) or voluntary.

- **Trauma movements:** These are movements connected to biological responses such as an impulse to flee, a galvanization to defend, a frozen stilling of the body, or facial expressions that placate a perceived threat. These movements are in service of the autonomic nervous system; when it is activated, the body responds with movements toward safety or against danger.

- **Developmental movements:** The natural physical movements and patterns of early developmental childhood, such as pushing, pulling, reaching, and swaying. These can include reflexive movements such as arching the back or the neck. Through these movements we learn about ourselves, other people, and the world. For example, when we reach toward our caregiver, their response will shape our beliefs about whether we can expect love and connection from others.

- **Relational movements:** These movements are in relation to another person, whether imagined or present. For example, a stretched-out hand toward the therapist can indicate a bid for connection.

Relational movements can also be with nature or elements, with the body moving in conscious response with their environment.

You'll want to track these qualities of movement:

- Reflexes and primitive defense responses connected to trauma experiences that are activating

- Truncated impulses such as fight, flight, and freeze

- A movement sequence that gets interrupted as the client processes (e.g., getting distracted, feeling stuck, or becoming overwhelmed by emotion)

- Orienting and defense responses that help settle the nervous systems

- The body response of "freeze" and any "no" movements

- Movements that serve as somatic resourcing and help the client feel safe, grounded, and connected

- Movements indicating well-being and pleasure in the body

- Movements that are playful and relational, showing a desire to connect socially

- Developmental movements that are in the body as unprocessed material

The worksheet *Tracking Internal Beliefs* is a helpful tool you may want to use again and again to track clients' movements.

Formula for Facilitating Movement

"The body is the vessel in which the transformation process takes place."

—James Hillman, *Suicide and the Soul*

Movement wants to be. It's as simple as that. Yet the thinking mind, the inhibitions of the body, emotional patterns, and physical pain or limitations can impact the motivation to move or bring up fear to start moving. Often clients feel self-conscious, ashamed, or like they do not know how to move. However, once they begin, they can feel a sense of freedom and experience new ways of exploring their body and psyche.

Your role is to facilitate and observe the process of moving. See yourself as a kind supporter, and bring to the movement exploration a mindful attitude. You want the client to notice and be with what they are doing and how it relates to the issues they are working on. Connect the client with the *how* and the *why* of their movement. Go slow, allow self-agency, track what comes up, and make contact.

GO SLOW

Encourage the client to become mindful of their movement, so that they can be with what is happening and discover the deeper meaning of their movements. Start by naming the movement and asking them to tune into it. You might say, "Your arm is rising up and swaying" or "There is a small movement in your foot right now." Note the simple description of the movement, with no comment on what it means at this time. You are simply fostering movement awareness in the present moment.

ALLOW SELF-AGENCY

Let the client be in control of their movement expression and pacing, and simply be with them. You can say, "Go at your own pace. See what feels right at this moment." You want to facilitate the unfolding of the movement, not make it into a performance or reenactment. Give the client self-control so they are more comfortable and willing to explore. Use encouraging statements such as "See what pace you want to move," "What wants to move next?" and "Go ahead and allow this movement to go wherever it wants to go."

TRACK WHAT COMES UP

Be present with what the client expresses. Be curious and attentive to the movement that is coming up. You can ask yourself: "What is the client's movement wanting to express? How is their movement supporting what is being said or not said?"

Remember that movement is an expression but also a story that is being told. It brings the client into an embodiment of what they are feeling and sensing. Track if the client gets overwhelmed or stuck in any way. You can simply remind them to slow down again. They can pause at any time. Bring movement awareness back—for example: "You stopped moving right there." You want the client to be mindful and be with their experience, not to be hijacked by states of high anxiety. When that comes up, you can always slow and pause and resource your client.

While the client is moving, hold back any comments about what the motion means. You want to simply encourage the movement for the sake of moving. The client needs to establish a connection with what that feels like and not be interrupted. Hold the energetic space for their exploration and track how they are expressing their movements. Notice what is being moved (or not moved) and how. Observe what needs attention, such as movements that seem to be connected to particular expressions; parts of the body or types of motions that the client is using repeatedly, or perhaps not using at all; or areas in which the client seems to be stuck or struggling. Save any verbal processing until after the exploration is done, at which point you can simply ask: "Do you want to sit down and talk about it?"

MAKE CONTACT WITH WHAT IS PRESENT

As you facilitate your client's movement exploration and verbally process with them afterward, do not impose your own interpretations on them. Simply name with nonjudgment and open curiosity what is occurring for the client and offer open-ended questions as needed. This allows the client to make meaning and learn to embody their own experience. You might say:

- "I noticed you were making a small movement with your right hand."
- "Did you notice that you were . . . as you talked about . . . ?"
- "If this feeling had a movement, what would it be?"
- "How would you express this image in movement?"
- "See if you can make a very small movement in your [*forehead, neck, hand, etc.*] that's very subtle and barely visible."
- "Go ahead and let that tremor movement go through."

Emotional Attunement

"The moving body is the conduit of our emotions and imagination."

—Manuela Mischke-Reeds

Emotional attunement is a fundamental tool for every therapist who wants to be empathetic and compassionate with their client. Our empathic attunement lets the client know that we understand their experience.

We can also attune somatically by learning to resonate through our own soma with the movement the client is expressing. This is a technique often referred to as *mirroring*. This technique can be helpful when you want to understand the client's experience more deeply and at the same time not get overwhelmed by their affect. Remember that we are movement, and when we are moving our bodies we process what is occurring.

The therapist often holds and waits, but this can cause tension and dysregulation to build up. We can use micro-movement to adjust and move without this being a distraction in the work. Use the exercise *Resonating Through Micro-Movements* when you want to gather direct information from your body. This is helpful not only during the session but also afterward as you process.

Tracking Internal Beliefs

PURPOSE

This worksheet will help you to track the beliefs the client is verbalizing when moving with any of the tools in this book. It will help you to see the main themes that are coming up and reflect on what some of the movements that are not clear yet could possibly mean. It can help you when you integrate the therapy process with your client by collecting the themes that are arising with the experience.

INSTRUCTIONS

As you record your observations and reflections on the client's movements, consider the following categories. You can also make copies of the template found at the end of these instructions to create your log.

- **Tools used:** Start with listing the name of the tool(s) used.

- **Client belief named:** List the issues and themes that come up while the client is moving. It could be what the client verbalizes, like "I feel so wooden and cold." Or you can write down keywords and any other associated beliefs, such as "emotionally frozen" or "fearful."

- **Movement qualities observed:** Write down what you see as they move—for example, upper arms held close to the body, breath limited to the upper chest, or small jerky movements. These notes will help you be more neutral when describing the movements when you reflect and integrate them together.

- **Client's debrief—short synopsis:** Jot down what you hear as core themes as the client makes connections and reflects on their experience. Listen carefully and write down the beliefs they actually express in their own words.

- **Belief indicators in debrief:** Jot down your thoughts and speculative ideas about the client's experience. For example, as the client talks about feeling wooden, you might note that you hear a tremble in her voice that indicates a held-back fear. This will help you to start making sense of deeper themes and experiences that are emerging but not yet fully in the client's awareness. Also write down what you picked up somatically in your own experience in relation to the client's journey.

- **Key beliefs to follow up:** Summarize the key beliefs that are emerging: what you witnessed, what the client shared, and what your intuitive sense is. Here you can note what you want to follow up with in subsequent sessions.

TIPS

Here are some helpful tips as you are tracking for movement:

- Go at the pace of the client. Study how they are moving to learn this language of their expression.

- Follow what wants to be known to the client.

- Slow down and get into an experiential mindset.

- Ask the client to slow down and get curious. Discover!

- Be ready to be with what comes up, as sometimes feelings, sensations, and memories can arise very quickly.

- Always ask if it's okay to stop or pause.

- As much as it is comfortable, do the movement with the client for a mutual connection or mirroring, or as emotional support. (This is discussed further in chapter 10.)

- See movement as an expression of who they are.

- Be extra sensitive to feelings of body shame and vulnerabilities arising.

- Create safety when self-conscious moments come up. Reframe your role as witnessing and being with the client, not looking at them.

- As you witness, also notice what is *not* moving. What parts of the body are still, held, or hidden? You can simply ask, "What else do you notice?"

Tools Used	Client Belief Named	Movement Qualities Observed	Client's Debrief—Short Synopsis	Belief Indicators in Debrief	Key Beliefs to Follow Up	Notes

Resonating Through Micro-Movements

PURPOSE

Use this technique when you want to gather more information from your own body in relation to your client's movement exercise exploration. As your client moves, you will do very small movements to attune to what you witness. You can use your somatic experience through movement to learn what the client is feeling, to understand your own somatic countertransference, to regulate your own inner state, and to communicate that you are with the client and attuning nonverbally. This is not a full mirroring exercise but rather a tool to begin to understand the inner somatic experience of the client.

INSTRUCTIONS

1. Settle yourself into a familiar grounding position, such as upright on your sitz bones or with your feet on the ground. This will help you feel the baseline from which you can explore.

2. As you witness or guide your client through their exercise and exploration, begin to mirror the qualities of their movement in your own body. For example, if the client is opening their held fists, you can mimic that motion by gently stretching your hands. If the client is doing a straightening of their spine and grounding their feet, you can mirror this directionality by lifting through the crown of your head and planting your feet consciously on the ground.

3. Make sure you are doing micro-movements that are barely visible. It's not about mimicking the client's motion; it's about sensing the quality and texture of the expression to attune and gather information. Find very, very small movements that mirror the qualities of the motions the client is inhabiting. This is not a full mirroring exercise. You are taking on these little pieces of textures and qualities to feel and resonate with the client's experience.

4. Take one quality at a time. Then release and notice when you feel you are getting information. That could be a feeling, a sense, an image, or a connection.

5. Be subtle so as not to derail the client's process. This is for you to learn and attune. Be receptive and listen to your own body as you do this as much as you can while being present with your client.

6. Repeat the micro-movement: take on one quality and mirror it in a very micro way, then drop it and notice:

   - What do you sense inside your body?
   - What information do you receive?
   - What overlap do you notice between what the client reports and your own experience?
   - Do you feel more empathy and compassion for your client?

REFLECTION

After the session, reflect on what you have learned about your own body in relation to your client's process. Consider the following prompts:

- When my client moved [*body part*] like [*quality of movement*], I saw and imagined . . .

- I noticed when I micro-mirrored, the client [*describe the movement*]. In my own body, I felt . . .

- I noticed that my feelings were . . .

- I noticed my connection with the client being . . .

- What I understand about their experience is . . .

- What I understand about my own movement experience is . . .

_____

_____

_____

_____

_____

_____

_____

_____

_____

_____

_____

_____

_____

_____

_____

CHAPTER 5

GUIDING MOVEMENT

"Emotions interpret the world for us."

—**Gabor Maté**, *The Myth of Normal*

As human beings, we develop and mature from infancy to childhood with our emotions, behaviors, and movements. We explore the early world of infancy through touch and all our senses. We learn to move our arms and legs in space lying on our backs, reaching for the loving faces of our parents. We learn to push up on our hands to lift our heads, orienting in the room around us. We tune into sounds and stimuli, reaching toward what makes us curious. We learn to roll, scoot, and crawl, to curl our toes under and create friction with the ground to propel ourselves across the carpet. Eventually, we discover the alignment within our bodies to push through our skeletal structure to learn to stand. We learn to add momentum to the standing body. We walk, then run, discovering the speed and power in our bodies.

We learn that movement goes in tandem with music as we sway to the rhythms of our cultures. We discover that fear and anger elicit powerful movements and feelings in the body, and we express these emotions through gestures, pushes, and pulls. We learn that the moving bodies around us have a powerful effect on how we move our own bodies in our environment.

We adapt in compromised bodies, finding creative ways to move around the world in wheelchairs, with crutches, and in confined small spaces. We observe the bodies of our families and society through our senses and learn what is acceptable or not, safe or not, through the restriction or liberation of their movements. We encounter the impact of stress, trauma, and pain in our bodies. We grapple with aging bodies that have limits and slowed moving capacities. In moving meditation we can feel the lineages of our ancestors in our bodies—all the silent imprints on our cellular bodies of their pain, pride, and trauma. We can feel, sense, and access these wisdoms through moving with our own bodies.

At every stage of the human developmental journey we are moving our bodies in relation to the environment and the planet. We are in moving relationships with others. It's the primary language of our senses and how we feel.

Developmental Movement Considerations

"The developmental process establishes the basic patterns of all our movement."

—Bonnie Bainbridge Cohen, *Sensing, Feeling and Action*

When we ask our client to engage consciously with movement, we are potentially meeting all their life stages and past experiences. This is a direct communication with how this human has moved in their life and wants to move forward at the same time. We could reawaken a sense of deep connection with a parent or a sense of being an infant, a young child, or a developing teenager. We can tap into these body memories through movement. It's a powerful tool.

To guide our clients safely and with meaningful outcomes, we want to observe some ground rules. Understanding that you are potentially tapping into this vast reservoir of life and memories, adopt these basic guidelines when guiding clients:

- Ask permission to introduce movement.

- Track and observe with compassion.

- Learn to read the body as a lived experience.

- Pay attention to the small movements in the body.

- Notice what movements are repeated.

- Bring a kind, warm, and gentle focus when you work with the body.

- Respect the client's no (and track for the unspoken no).

- Honor the client's boundaries; never push or impose an agenda.

- Stay with your own experience and do not interpret their experience.

- Track gestures, postures, and facial expressions as the silent language of the soma.

- Accept what the client's body knowledge brings forth.

The client can easily feel vulnerable and raw in their experience, and the aim is to have the patterns be discovered with new information, choices, and healing. Encourage them with statements such as "You are welcome here," "You can safely explore," "It's okay to just play and sense," and "You are safe right now." Find a balance where you listen, observe, and gently encourage exploration, especially when you notice any contraction or confusion in the movements. Encourage the client to slow down, orient in the room, and make sure this feels okay.

Often floor work means the client is moving on the ground, which can feel particularly vulnerable; they may be doing sensitive infant movements, for example. You want to come down to the ground with the client, as it could feel awkward or even threatening for them to be watched by someone who is standing over them. Issues of power dynamics can arise. Make sure you minimize these by coming down to their level. Keep a professional but warm distance so that the client feels spaciousness to explore but doesn't feel observed. Acknowledge that you will transition down to the floor—you can say, "I am going to come down on the floor with you. I will sit here as you explore. I will hold the safe space for you. I am not going anywhere and will be fully present with you." This helps the client learn to trust and explore.

Physicalizing What Is Felt Inside Somatically

"But all my life—so far—I have loved best how the flowers rise and open, how the pink lungs of their bodies enter the fire of the world and stand there shining and willing—the one thing they can do before they shuffle forward into the floor of darkness, they become the trees."

—Mary Oliver, "Moccasin Flowers"

Movement is a powerful ally in working somatically. Some clients might find it challenging to sense and feel their inner experience, and movement can be an externalization of what is happening inside. By guiding the client to first become aware of their movement and then to physicalize a feeling or sensation through movement, you are helping the client to feel more and to become clear about the feeling they are having.

Some feelings can be difficult to express, but if you invite movement to that feeling it will give it shape and form that is more tangible. Likewise, movement is often accompanied by a feeling, emotion, or bodily sensation. Even the absence of a movement *is* a movement. This is especially true when the client is feeling frozen, overwhelmed, or stuck. You can facilitate that feeling into a movement expression, helping the client to befriend what was challenging at first. Suggesting movement, or even mirroring movement, can be helpful for clients who feel shut down. Their mirror neurons will perceive the movement and it will have an influence, even if they can't grasp it at that very moment. How you physicalize your presence is an important part of introducing movement into the work.

Here are some considerations to keep in mind:

1. Learn to track movement *as* the client tells their story. Notice when and what kind of movement goes with that.

2. Offer movement opportunities when you see them. Invite the client into what is already there.

3. Offer the exercises with an open and inquisitive mindset.

4. Practice movement for yourself and learn the exercise from the inside out.

5. Be creative and tailor these practices to the needs of your clients.

6. Help physicalize what can't be spoken and offer compassionate witnessing when the client has the courage to do so.

What Is This Current Movement?

PURPOSE

This is a general protocol that you can use when you are exploring a movement that is arising spontaneously, assisting the client to move through a body memory, or helping the client to self-regulate.

Make sure you remind the client to slow down and feel in control of their moving experience.

INSTRUCTIONS

1. Invite the client to explore a movement.

2. Remind the client that they can pause, be silent, and open their attention at any time.

3. Go ahead and start with the movement that is here. Ask them, *What movement goes with this experience?*

4. Gently start by mirroring the client's movements to create safety and connection. Check in with the client by normalizing what arises. Assist the client in deepening into the moving process by using this gentle invitation: *Go ahead and see what movement feels just right. See if you can stay with the movement that is arising right now. Allow yourself to explore, and see where this leads you. Trust these motions to guide you.*

5. When the client is in the moving process, indicate that you will stop mirroring and that you will hold silent space. Make sure you are staying on their level—standing when they are standing and going down to the floor when they do—so the client does not feel observed. At this stage you want them to be immersed in their moving experience and not rely on you. Track your client's movement as if it is a language that is being painted, sung, and written in human motion. Soften your eyes and let go of catching every detail.

6. If the client has emotional or physical tension, you can offer these choice points:

   - **Something else?** *What is another movement that goes with _____?* Allow the client to express it and move with it. Find the symbolic nature of the movement.

   - **Relax into it:** Offer an instruction: *Allow yourself to relax into this moment, into that tension. You can use the breath, a small micro-movement . . . what allows you right now to relax into this stuckness?*

   - **Pause:** You can say, *Take the pause, let open attention be here right now, and allow yourself to wait . . . open your inner lens of awareness wide . . .*

7. Explore until you see a natural closing or the client wants to pause.

8. Ask them to quietly harvest and receive the learning from their movement exploration. You might invite them to sit or lie down. They can change body posture and position to be more receptive.

9. Then indicate slowly that it's time to transition; be very present as they do so. Welcome the client with an open, curious, and neutral attitude.

10. Debrief the experience, and let the client talk first. Offer only a few key observations. Don't interpret. Keep your observations short, precise, and connected with what you witnessed and what you imagined. Practice observing *for* the client, not sharing your own experience.

11. Debrief and reflect together on the following key takeaways. You can have the client write these down first and have them reflect before debriefing the experience.

    - What shift happened today in your body?

    - What is important about this exploration?

    - What learning are you taking with you?

Finding the Moving Body

PURPOSE

This exercise is to help the client find their moving body. Here you can encourage the client to notice the movements they want to explore. The main objective is to teach the idea that there is a moving body at all times and, just like a stream of thoughts, we can follow a movement expression. A movement can have its own silent narrative. You can start by observing a movement in the client and asking them if they want to explore that further. Or you can suggest a movement that goes with what they are currently talking about. This will shift the client from talking about feelings to sensing into the present moment. Make this initially very doable and small, to lower any barriers of shame or self-consciousness.

INSTRUCTIONS

1. Notice and name a movement you observed in the client.

2. Ask: *Would you like to explore the movement you just did?*

3. After you get permission, gently guide the client. You can say:

   - *Notice that movement and repeat it a couple of times.*

   - *Now see if that movement has a direction. Does it want to go up, down, et cetera?*

   - *Repeat the sequence you just did, from where you started, to what the next movement was.*

   - *Pause and sense your body right now. Allow yourself to get mindful and notice your body right now . . . what are you noticing?*

4. When the exploration has come to a close, invite the client to write down what came up for them.

REFLECTION

Afterward, ask your client the following questions and discuss:

- What comes up for you right now as you reflect?

- What part of your body is in your awareness right now?

- What did this movement connect you with?

- What was it like to follow the movement?

Following an Impulse

PURPOSE

This exercise is helpful to learn about impulses in the body and how to be with them without being overwhelmed or needing to act on them. The body has many impulses that we might not be aware of, such as a twitch, a jerky motion, a sense of wanting to move, or a micro-motion that we are feeling. An impulse can be highly charged with emotions or a story that is embedded into the body. Impulses can be connected with interrupted movements or behaviors when we have experienced trauma; perhaps we had an impulse to fight or run away, but we could not, and so the impulse was overridden. When we connect with the movement impulses in the body we can connect with body memories directly. The client can feel in control by mindfully exploring an impulse toward its completion.

INSTRUCTIONS

As you guide your client through these steps, make sure to pace them mindfully. Have your client study the impulses, not just do them. *Being with* the impulse is the important part here. Keep in mind that you're speaking with the moving body, not just giving instructions. Go slow, take pauses, and really observe the body. Give the client the space to feel it. Say:

1. *Notice an impulse in your body that you want to explore. Place your attention on this impulse; you might want to close your eyes. Draw your attention inside and feel the impulse in the body.*

2. *Let that impulse become a small movement . . . move mindfully and notice anything that comes with this impulse. If there are feelings that go with the impulse, let them be there, but let your main attention be on the impulse.*

3. *Continue following the impulse. You might notice another impulse that comes after that. Slow down enough so you can be present with these continuous impulses. Let go of any narrative and explore one impulse moving into another one.*

4. *For a few moments, let yourself simply follow the impulses and see how they connect to one another. Take your time and discover.*

5. *Then find a natural resting and sense in your body. What is present right now?*

REFLECTION

With your client, discuss and reflect on the impulse and how it has changed.

Noticing and Addressing the "No" in the Body

PURPOSE

In any of these exercises you might find that the client feels discomfort, or the body says *no*. Even if the client starts with good intentions, the body can say no. Learning to read the no is very important. The no can have many meanings, and it's a truly wise part coming forth. Support your client to accept this knowledge and to embody the no. You want to honor and work with that no in a mindful way. Give the client choice points so they can explore the no in a creative way, talk about it, move it, or simply stop.

INSTRUCTIONS

1. When the client is moving, watch for common body indicators of a no, such as:

    - Bracing of muscles

    - Tightness in the body

    - Gaze either averted or cast down, not relational

    - Tightness around the mouth and eyes

    - Breath being held

    - Movement being done without awareness—no real connection with the actual movements

2. Whenever you track these indicators of "no," you can engage the client by saying, *I am noticing* [describe the body cues]. *What do you notice right now?* or *Is there a "no" that you are feeling in your body right now? How do you notice that?*

3. Then you can offer some choices:

    - *You could be with this no by moving the quality of it through your hands.*

    - *You can pause and notice the no and see what needs to happen next.*

    - *You can stop and we can talk about what is coming up for you.*

4. Move on by saying, *Notice what happens with the no inside as you hear these choices. What do you notice? Is there another way you would like to be with this no?*

5. It the client chooses to move the no, you can ask:

    - *What movement goes with the no?*

    - *What rhythm does the no have?*

- *What feelings are here?*
- *Where does the no movement want to go?*

6. Ask your client to write down what they discovered by responding to the following prompts:
   - When I feel a no in my body, I need to . . .
   - When I sense a no, I have the choice of . . .
   - When I express my no, I discover I can . . .
   - My no means that . . .
   - When I feel connected to my no, I can . . .
   - Here is where my yes is . . .

Finding Your Baseline—Mindful Moving

PURPOSE

This exercise is a good precursor to any movement exploration. You are taking a baseline of where your client currently is and helping them to sense into their moving body, one breathing cycle at a time. This exercise is typically done standing.

INSTRUCTIONS

Guide your client mindfully. Pace these directions slowly, following your client's needs:

1. *Find a comfortable standing position.*

2. *Take some deeper breaths that expand your belly and your chest.*

3. *Notice how the breaths begin to create a subtle movement in the body.*

4. *Begin to express the rhythm of breathing by lightly raising your arms alongside your body, as if you are spreading imaginary wings. With the inhale you raise your arms slightly . . . and with the exhale you bring your arms down.*

5. *Now begin another cycle of inhaling, slightly raising your arms . . . and exhaling, lowering your arms. Bring mindful attention to this movement.*

6. *Every time you complete a breathing cycle, rest your arms, breathe naturally, and check in with your body. This is your baseline.*

7. *Now, let's check in. How do you sense yourself now? What is present in your experience?*

8. *Continue a few more breaths like that. Pause after three cycles and check in. Notice what changes as you do this. Make sure you do this mindfully. Rest in the stillness and notice what you feel.*

9. *Now stand quietly for a moment and listen to your body with openness.*

REFLECTION

After the exercise, invite your client to respond to the following prompts, either out loud or in writing.

- Before I started moving, I felt _____ in my body.

- Now I feel _____

What Movement Goes with This Feeling?

PURPOSE

This exercise is an easy entry into working with **movement**.

INSTRUCTIONS

Simply ask the client to bring movement to what they are experiencing: *What movement goes with this feeling?* This will help them to externalize what they are feeling inside. You can use the following prompts to gently guide them and write down for the client what they're experiencing as you're discussing:

- *What is the feeling that you're having right now?*
- *What is the movement that wants to be expressed with the feeling you are having right now?*
- *What is the movement that wants to happen next?*
- *What is the movement that you are afraid to express?*
- *Go ahead and move with that feeling right now. How does it feel to move?*

REFLECTION

Afterward, discuss together the connections between the movements and the feelings that were discovered.

CHAPTER 6

SOCIAL LOCATIONS AND SYSTEMS

"Unhealed trauma acts like a rock thrown into a pond; it causes ripples
that move outward, affecting many other bodies over time."

—**Resmaa Menakem**, *My Grandmother's Hands*

Because moving enhances self-awareness, it can bring forth sensitivities about social location. *Social location* refers to a person's position in society, where they stand in the community in which they engage. The position is based on many factors, including history, gender, racial identity, social status, level of education, age, and ethnicity. It's also influenced by the systems in which they live, such as their family system. For example, if the client grew up in a household that was strict or did not allow for expression, it could result in the client feeling more self-conscious about how to move their body, and limit how free or at ease they might feel to move in public spaces. Social location can also bring forth inner critics and judgments about one's body shape, size, and appearance. It sometimes dictates what is considered acceptable in terms of how the body moves.

The inquiry into one's social location—both the client's and the therapist's—can come up at any time in the therapy work. Because movement trauma therapy work can be evocative, bringing forth feelings that were not consciously recognized at first, the discomfort that can arise with one's own social location or being impacted by the other person's social location can become a theme. Expect this to come up, and embrace it.

We can think of social location in two ways: how we perceive ourselves and how others perceive us. Others' perceptions can set up expectations; for example, I am white, bicultural, bilingual, an immigrant with a privileged educational background, a somatic psychotherapist, a dancer and a mover who is able bodied and comfortable moving in her body. If I have a client from a very different background who is not comfortable moving due to their cultural and societal upbringing and trauma in their body, it can set up feelings of shame, pressure to move a certain way, or feeling othered and even unwelcome.

We can't change our history, where we come from, or how our ancestors lived. Our social location is an imprint and shaped our worldview when we were growing up. But we can learn about this imprint, become aware of how we are perceived by others, consciously strive to be inclusive and trauma-informed, and not assume that the norms of our own social location are universal.

For therapists reflecting on their own social location and the imprinted messages around somatic knowledge of one's body, it is important to explore the client's comfort or discomfort with movement, including past trauma and messages the client has received about whether and how it's okay to move.

For instance, I might signal unconsciously that my ease with movement should be felt by everyone and not recognize that my client feels ashamed, frozen, or simply uncertain of how to move their body. We all carry deep societal, cultural, and trauma messages around how alive and embodied we are allowed to be. When engaging with movement tools, we will inevitably discover deep unconscious themes of the past. Our history is held in our body memories, and the trauma of families and intergenerational patterns can surface vividly in the moving experience. This conversation touches on history, family roots, and the shadow of our ancestors.

Our social location affects how we hold the role as a therapist, our sense of power and authority, the social norms we assume, how we speak to our clients, and how we move in relation to them. How we move in the space in our office is tracked by the client. Depending on their social location and how it differs from your own, a client might feel very comfortable or very uncomfortable about how you physically move in the space. This is being tracked by the nervous system in milliseconds and translates into the client's sense of "I belong here" or "the therapist doesn't get me."

I encourage you to take some time to reflect on your social location identification and social imprints, and consider how to make interactions with your clients safer. The more aware we are of our own social location, and the more we engage with our own history without judgment but with kindness, the more we invite a somatic safety with our client. They can feel and sense if you are comfortable in your own skin. When they come across their own internal somatic messages or wonder about your different social location from theirs, it can become a topic to be worked with and enrich the therapy process.

Tips When Exploring Social Location and Systems

This is a sensitive and deep process that will involve much exploration and practice. Here are some helpful tips to keep in mind as you approach this topic:

- Be kind to yourself.

- Be curious and refrain from making any judgments. Stay open to learning.

- Remember there's nothing here to be mastered. This exploration aims to increase awareness within so that you can receive the client's struggle with trauma in relation to their ancestors and history, and discover how it wants to heal today.

- Be a beginner in this social location learning even if you believe you know all about your own experience. Shunryu Suzuki Roshi, a famous Zen master, said: "In the beginner's mind there are many possibilities, but in the expert's there are few." Even if we are experts in facilitating deep therapy processes, when it comes to our own history and identification, we can only know as much as our current awareness allows. In 10 years you will know more and have a different perception.

- Be deeply yourself and be open to how you are being perceived so that you can make respectful choices in client engagement.

- Notice if you tense up and messages of "I am wrong," "I can't get it right," fear, and so forth come up. Notice, relax, and remind yourself that this *is* the learning.

Social Location in Movement

PURPOSE

Use this reflection for yourself or offer it as a tool for your client, when appropriate. Clients can do this alone first, and then discuss it. The purpose is to examine your own social location, especially when you're working with a client whose experience and background are different from yours. Consider this exercise when you notice the client is hesitant to move their body or is holding back because they feel unsafe, unsure, or that they're doing it wrong; this can indicate a perception that your social location is restricting their process in some way.

INSTRUCTIONS

Complete each statement on this form or in your journal.

- I am struggling because the client is perceiving me as _____.

- I notice in my struggle that my body does _____.

- I am noticing that I identify _____.

- When I am being seen as _____, I feel _____.

- I acknowledge that my client sees me as _____.

- I am opening myself to this perception and learning that _____.

- I sense my body being _____.

- I see myself now as _____.

- I connect with who I am without judgment when _____.

- Any other reflections:

  _____

  _____

  _____

  _____

After this reflection, allow yourself to gently breathe and move in any way that feels supportive and resourcing. Then notice what has shifted.

Exploring the Shaping of Systems

PURPOSE

In this exercise, you will help your client explore the shapes that have shaped them. When we explore themes of family and ancestral lineage, the movement language can be very helpful. We often don't have direct knowledge of our lineage, only hunches, fragments of stories, a feeling. It's easy then to dismiss our experience and not become aware of how these imprints are living in our soma. Movement becomes a direct route to explore these shapes and messages, and make conscious what your client has felt and sensed but didn't have a language for.

INSTRUCTIONS

Encourage the client to trust their movement experience. You can offer simple instructions such as:

- *Allow this movement to happen.*
- *Connect this image to a movement right now.*
- *Follow that shape, one breath at a time.*
- *Stay with the shaping as it changes . . . sense and see.*
- *See if you can follow this shape to its natural conclusion.*

This exercise is not about right or wrong, or finding a definitive truth. It's about exploring the shapes we are conscious of and letting the movement reveal its meaning. See if you can adopt a very accepting and curious stance as your client explores. Guide them by saying:

1. *Think of a theme you want to explore about the family, lineage, and history that have shaped you. It could be "the shape of my family," or "my shape in the family," or "my ancestor's shape." It can come from a picture you have seen or an image you hold of the person or people you are working with. Keep it simple.*

2. *Now, enter into a shape. For example, it could be a standing posture with a hunched-over shoulder and collapsed chest, or a clenched fist with the rest of the body relaxed—any shape that feels right to you in this moment.*

3. *Hold that shape. Breathe now, slowly . . . you can close your eyes if you would like.*

4. *Let that shape sink into your awareness. Take your time.*

5. *Make a commitment to explore this shape, without judgment and with curiosity. You can say inside: "I am open to exploring the shape within."*

6. *Use the breath to feel and sense your way into that shape. Notice how the breath begins to initiate a very small motion in relation to that shape.*

7. *Feel, sense, and move very, very incrementally within that shape.*

8. *Make sure you are not directing this from your planning mind but are truly sensing yourself through the soma.*

9. *Take your time . . . slow down . . . move one moment at a time.*

10. *Let that shape teach you about how you have been shaped. You will follow the impulses or inner imagery that arises; feelings might come up.*

11. *Don't overthink. Let the moving experience inform you.*

12. *Stay with it and see what is happening now. Trust what comes up. You might not make sense of it right away. Trust . . .*

Follow this experience until there is a natural pause, insight, or conclusion. Then, ask your client to sit quietly and take 10 to 15 minutes to answer the following questions by journaling or discussing. Have your client focus on becoming aware of how the soma has been impacted by the shape of their family, culture, system, history, and so forth, so that they can own what needs to be and let go of what is no longer needed. (See the next exercise, *The Shape Release Process*.)

- How did the shape show up?

- What was the pathway?

- What were the textures, feelings, and sensations?

- What was the message attached to the shape?

- What changed or got clear as you moved with that shape?

- What was the power of that shape?

- What serves this shape?

- What no longer serves this shape?

- What are the limiting beliefs that have been connected with this shape?

The Shape Release Process

PURPOSE

This is a follow-up exercise to *Exploring the Shaping of Systems*. In this exercise your client will focus on consciously releasing the shapes that no longer serve them. This practice will need to be repeated, as shapes from the past have powerful societal reinforcers. Over time, your client will discover that these shapes are not just external but internal—they're shapes we hold and live by. With growing awareness, your client can start noticing when these shapes return as triggers or reminders of the past. Make this a practice; over time the shapes that no longer serve your client will make way for the shapes your client wants to inhabit.

INSTRUCTIONS

When your client has identified a shape that is no longer serving them, encourage them to move with that shape, explore, and change it. Strong feelings and sensations may arise; encourage the client to move right through it. Explain that this is not the time to analyze, and encourage them to trust the moving shape that can be transformed. Guide them to find a new shape. You can ask questions such as *What is the shape that wants to be? Where is the new shape living? How does the shaping of the past serve you and where does it want to go now? What is next?*

Set an Intention

Read the following lines to your client and invite them to spontaneously fill in the blanks out loud as they explore the shape physically:

- *I am letting go of the shape of _____.*
- *I acknowledge the shape of _____ showing up in my body as _____ [a feeling or sensation].*
- *I no longer want to be the carrier of this shape or _____.*

Shifting the Shape

Truly immerse your client in the play and exploration of the shape they identified. It can be quite literally holding the shape and then adding to it or changing it. There might be laughter, play, anger, fear, trembling, and shaking—encourage the client to let all these movements move through as the pathway to releasing the hold of the old shape and associated feelings. Encourage your client to experiment with textures, pacing, breath, sound, and following new motions that feel pleasant, powerful, and so forth. Offer the following prompts and have your client fill in the blanks aloud while moving:

- *Take on that familiar shape and name it out loud.*

- *Add one motion that changes it . . . what is its name?*

- *Add a sound or breath that changes it . . . what is its name?*

- *I am discovering that when I move with the old shape, I can _____.*

- *I am learning that the shape can change into _____.*

HARVEST THE CHANGE: CALLING IN THE UNFAMILIAR AND NEW

To process and integrate the experience, have the client discuss or journal about the following prompts:

- I am feeling _____ in my body right now.

- I am committing to nourishing this _____ [*action, intention, feeling*] as a daily practice for myself.

- I am calling in the qualities of _____ to support this change of shape.

- When I recognize the old shape, I will _____ [*describe an antidote you discovered, such as a movement, image, thought, or resource that you will apply*].

- I give thanks to _____.

CHAPTER 7

TRAUMA–SENSITIVE RESOURCING MOVEMENTS

"Movers tend to explore a very wide range of uroboric self-holding. We see all kinds of patterns: one hand holding the other; thumb-holding; arm(s) wrapping around the torso to hold rib(s), elbow(s), hip(s), knee(s), foot or feet. All of these seem reminiscent of those earliest body experiences when we at first unintentionally find, then lose, then find again—and gradually discover what it is to hold and be held."

—**Joan Chodorow,** *Dance Therapy and Depth Psychology*

Somatic resourcing is an essential technique for helping the client settle their nervous system, move through difficult inner places such as trauma-activated emotions and memories, and learn to self-regulate their emotions. In somatic resourcing the client is actively engaged in their body process and places their attention on their sensations and feelings to ground, settle, and navigate through their inner states.

Resourcing movements are a subset of somatic resourcing to aid the client in finding self-regulated places within their body. They are movements that will ground and help the client to feel embodied, safe, and aware. Engaging the moving body can be helpful for clients who struggle with sensing into their bodies. By starting to acknowledge what is present—inner discomfort, feeling emotionally stuck, frustration, nervousness, anxiety, or heaviness, as examples—and then engage movement with the experience, the client is often able to settle the discomfort and become more aware of their body.

The idea of "moving through" a challenging somatic place can be very useful for clients. It's an active participation that can feel empowering. Encourage your client to feel into movements that feel resourcing for them. For some clients, being in more action-oriented movement engages the sympathetic nervous system into feeling they are mobilizing and in control. For others, moving slowly and mindfully to befriend their triggered body feelings engages the parasympathetic nervous system into a more measured response that does not overwhelm.

Resourcing movements can be:

- Grounding motions, such as placing the feet on the ground or stomping to feel the connection with the ground beneath

- Settling nervous system activation by using awareness and specific breaths to soothe and settle, one breath cycle at a time

- Stabilizing high activation and fear states by slowly moving and allowing shaking, tremors, sweat, and heat in the body to dissipate with control and self-agency

- Mindfully moving the body and being supported to alleviate body discomfort

- Helping to deepen into active resting states by taking a nourishing, comforting body position, such as lying on one's side

- Eliciting the ventral vagal social engagement system through playful interaction and engaging curiosity to discover what works

Tracking Movements Toward Resourcing

"There is a rhythmic interchange between action and quiet receptivity, between dream-like states and consciousness, between intuition and the world of the senses, between image and concretisation, between abandonment and control, between individual and shared reality."

—Bonnie Meekums, *Dance Movement Therapy*

We all have capacities for self-regulation within us. We learn self-regulation skills early in our core regulating relationships with our parents. Research into social connections shows us that when we feel socially connected, we gain access to our inner connection and feel a sense of belonging and thriving (Schultz et al., 2016; Sippel et al., 2015; Bryant, 2016). When we're disconnected, the opposite is true: without any social interaction, the self-regulating capacities diminish. When we feel disconnected, lonely, or frightened we have a sense of not belonging to our own soma. This is a phenomenon we often encounter in different kinds of trauma, such as developmental/attachment trauma, relational or community trauma, or complex PTSD.

We are sensing creatures, and, in this social engagement system of connection, we use our eyes, voice, touch, facial movements, and whole body to send and receive signals of safety and connection. As therapists, we want to bring our clients into self-regulating capacities through resourcing techniques to help them to remember their inner wellspring. They do this by exploring somatic resources that move them out of a dorsal vagal or sympathetic response into a more connected ventral vagal response. Movement is the conduit to move through these different autonomic nervous system states into a more connected sense of self.

Our entire nervous system is in constant motion. We respond and move with our environment. We track and notice the facial expressions of others and respond to their anger, disapproval, or friendliness through our body. We relax in nature and grieve when nature is hurt. We resonate deeply with the dynamic tones and textures of our human world as well as our natural world. We are in constant exchange, body to body, breath to breath, and movement to movement.

Becoming aware of when we feel safe and connected and when we do not is an essential skill when healing from trauma. That internal knowledge becomes the base from which the client can feel themselves and the impact other people's feelings and expressions have on their soma and psyche.

The moving body always gives us clues into these resourcing capacities. For example, a repetitive movement of pushing away or a small shaking can be connected to by adding a regulating breath and slowing down the movement in the body. As therapists, we have two choices of how we can resource the client's experience. We can guide them through an experience and have the client discover these resources as they explore. Or we can track for opportunities in the body where the client wants to connect but just doesn't know how yet. (See the exercise *Tracking Movements Toward Resourcing*).

When you are tracking your client going into a parasympathetic dorsal vagal response, such as freezing or numbness, you can ask them, "What small motion could help you to reconnect with a resource right now?" In the therapy work you always want to look for the opportunities where the client organically wants to connect with some internal resource. Feelings of warmth, calm, and social engagement can be externalized with a movement. This can bring awareness that somatic resources are available and the client has access to them. In the moments of somatic connection, you help the client build confidence in their own somatic resources.

Fascia Awareness

"I am convinced that for every physical non-yielding condition there is a psychic counterpart in the unconscious mind, corresponding exactly to the degree of the physical manifestation."

—Milton Trager

Fascia awareness plays an important role in somatic trauma therapy work. Fascia is a weblike structure that envelops our organs, muscles, bones, blood vessels, and nerve fibers. It's a sheet of stringy connective tissue made of collagen fibers. Think of having a thick inner suit that makes sure your muscles, bones, and organs are encased and provides you with fluid motions in the body. It creates an internal scaffold or support for the overall structure of the body. Because fascia touches every system and has nerves, it also provides a sensitive internal feedback system for the body. Fascia has more than 200 million nerve endings and more sensory neurons than motor neurons. It aids communication within the body, through the vagus nerve from body to brain in a bidirectional way. Fascia is also intertwined with the endocrine system by transmitting hormones such as estrogen, insulin, adrenaline, GABA, and neurotransmitters such as serotonin and dopamine.

When we have healthy fascia, it is slippery and smooth and eases the tension in the muscles as we move and stretch. Through micro channels, the primo vascular system, subtle fluid energies (primo fluids) are distributed throughout the body, reducing inflammation (Chikly et al., 2016). When we move and breathe, the fascia appropriately processes stressors by keeping itself smooth. With injury to the body or chronic emotional patterns, the fascia hardens. Layers of fascia build up to create a density in the cartilage of the connective tissue, which increases inflammation and other chronic pain issues (Avila Gonzalez et al., 2018).

When we experience a trauma stressor and freeze or faint, this unprocessed response can get stuck in the body. The result is that we no longer have a rhythmic expansion and contraction of our smooth muscle and fascia fibers, and build up a density in the tissues. Repeated muscle contraction from stress responses can result in tightening of the fascia and chronic pain such as myofascial pain syndrome. When the fascia is not healthy, it becomes thick, sticky, and tight, and creates pain in the body. The emotional and sensory experience is often of feeling thick, dense, or emotionally and somatically disconnected.

Fascia pain can be relieved when the body moves intentionally. When doing trauma release work, we want to include fascia awareness, as the chronic patterns can get activated through stress and habitual movement patterns do not include diverse enough movement.

When the client first begins to move intentionally, the dense fascia can feel as if they are moving through molasses and it takes effort to feel the body as fluid and smooth. By understanding that they are moving through the thickness of the fascia layers and are waking the body's inherent connective tissue to communicate again, they can develop a mental framework for these heavy or dense sensations they are feeling.

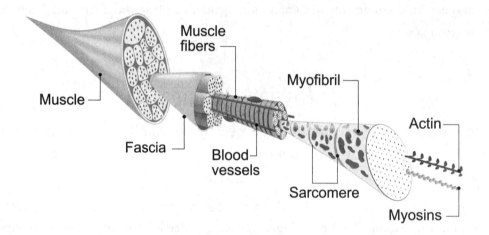

Pandicular Movement

"I believe cats to be spirits come to earth. A cat, I am sure,
could walk on a cloud without coming through."
—attributed to Jules Verne

Think of a cat as it stretches and yawns, releasing the tension after a nice nap. These are involuntary movements that mark the transition between sleeping and waking the body for action. Pandiculation is different from simply stretching; when we stretch we are more passive and waiting for the stretch sensation to take hold. In pandiculation, we are actively engaging and participating with the motion. Pandiculation restores smooth muscle function, releases tension, and induces a sense of well-being. We will often do an unconscious pandiculation when we wake up and the body has the urge to stretch; yawning often comes along with these movements. For these reasons, pandiculation is often referred to as a whole-body yawning.

By consciously using movements that pandiculate, we can calm the nervous system and instill a sense of healing. Pandicular movement is a kind of stretching and contracting that works with the fascia directly and helps metabolize the emotional trauma stored in the fascia. With gentle touch, intentional movement, and breath awareness, we can learn to unwind these tensions and patterns in the fascia and muscle system.

Tracking Movements Toward Resourcing

PURPOSE

In this exercise you are bringing awareness to the different nervous system states and what you can do to move out or stay with the nervous system states you are sensing. It's important to track what kinds of movement are helpful so that you can call on them when needed.

INSTRUCTIONS

Answer the questions on the lines below or in your journal to identify the key movements that can move you into or out of stress-response states.

My Center: Where I Feel Safe, Calm, and Socially Connected

How do I move toward inner safety?

_____

_____

What movement can help me stay here?

_____

_____

My Activated State: Mobilized for Fight or Flight

What movement helps me mobilize toward action?

_____

_____

What movements help me defend myself?

_____

_____

My Coping State: Immobilized, Withdrawn, or Collapsed

What movements help me hide?

_____

_____

What movements help me beyond the freeze?

_____

_____

The Three Arrows: Back into Your Center

PURPOSE

Discover what movements are most resourcing for you when you drift out of your center. You are training yourself to recognize drifting and practice returning to your center when you are emotionally activated. Repeat this exercise often, so that you can use it in the moment when you catch yourself drifting.

INSTRUCTIONS

In your journal or in the illustration, respond to the following questions.

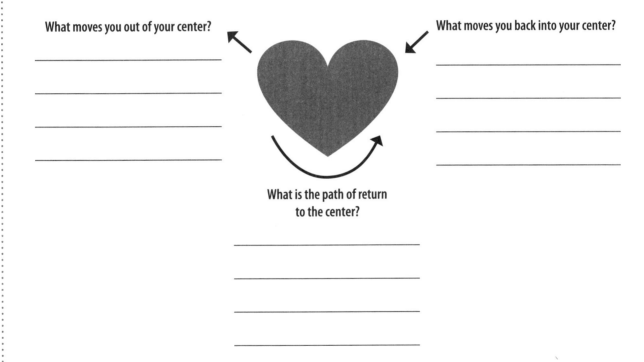

What moves you out of your center?

_____

_____

_____

_____

What moves you back into your center?

_____

_____

_____

_____

What is the path of return to the center?

_____

_____

_____

_____

After you have journaled, take a standing position and find a movement that goes with each of the arrows.

1. **What moves you out of your center?** Make a motion that symbolizes when you lose your center. Notice the speed and quality of this motion.

2. Pause and feel your body right now after having done that movement.

3. **What moves you back into your center?** Now make a motion that symbolizes how to come back to your center. Spend some time repeating that movement.

4. Pause and feel your body now. What do you notice?

5. **What is the path of return to the center?** Repeat the return movement and slow it down so you can notice how your pathway actually inflates. Mindfully follow the movement so you can remember this pathway.

After you have explored these different movements, return to your journal or use the space below. Write about what you have learned about returning to your center, to yourself.

_____

_____

_____

_____

_____

_____

_____

_____

_____

_____

_____

Gentle Rocking for Inner Calm

PURPOSE

This is a centering and regulating exercise to establish a sense of inner calm, balance, and safety. Use it when your client needs to return to their baseline. This is an excellent precursor to the other movement exercises in this book, particularly those in chapter 10, which explores movement in relation.

TIPS

If you have a rocking chair or a bouncy ball, this exercise can be done sitting, which can be helpful when there is a fear of falling or of body compromise when standing. Also, it's ideal to introduce this exercise in session, with you guiding; then it may be assigned as homework as needed.

INSTRUCTIONS

Guide your client through the following script:

1. *Start standing, in a relaxed posture, with your knees slightly bent.*

2. *You might want to have your eyes open, and cast them downward to bring your attention inward. Closing your eyes might impact your balance.*

3. *Tune in. What is your body feeling right now?*

4. *Place one or both hands on your heart.*

5. *Breathe calmly into the hands, with a slight emphasis on the exhale.*

6. *Then move your body gently back and forth so you feel a sense of rocking.*

7. *This is a very small rocking motion; you want your knees to be very soft.*

8. *You can explore either side-to-side or back-and-forth rocking. Tune into what your body feels more comfortable with.*

9. *Find a rhythm that feels soothing to you, that you can be with for a few minutes. Make the movement small enough so you get a sense of gentle rocking.*

10. *Imagine you are being rocked by a kind and benevolent movement.*

11. *[After 5 minutes] Pause the rocking and stand still. Sense into your body right now. Quietly ask yourself:*

    - *What is my body feeling now?*

    - *How connected do I feel?*

    - *How safe do I feel right now?*

REFLECTION

Have your client respond to the previous questions in their journal. You can also ask: *What does it mean to come back to your baseline? How does the rocking bring you there? Were there any images that came with that?*

Pandicular Movement

PURPOSE

Introducing the client to pandiculation has two aims: teaching them to actively initiate the movement to regulate and restore, and encouraging them to pay attention in daily life when the movement urges of the body are occurring. This is important, as the awareness that the body needs a reset is a body communication to heed. If the client's habit is to override cues that restoration is needed, such as by pushing the body, the awareness to take a "time out" to feel and sense a deep stretch within is powerful learning.

TIPS

Encourage movements that feel pleasurable, such as twists, unusual movements, or whatever happens spontaneously. Encourage the client to experiment; they might be shy at first, and you might need to mirror and do this with them. Be aware that you want to be supportive but not pushy. Use language such as: *Go ahead and follow what feels just right . . . as you sense this movement, see if you can go until there is true satisfaction in that stretch and contract.* As much playfulness as they allow will help this process.

INSTRUCTIONS

Introduce the client to pandiculation by supporting the physical movement with an image; a cat or dog stretching and yawning is often a good start. Emphasize to the client that these movements are about following whatever the body needs, meaning they can simply be with it, allow it, and linger in the aftereffects. If the movement results in the client feeling a rush of sensations and well-being, you want to celebrate this. It can be quite powerful to "feel alive" after feeling a shutdown in the body. Process what came up and how the body is feeling now.

If at any time the client wants to stop, pause and encourage them to be in open attention to notice. Often clients need a couple of these stretches and then a pause to acclimate and build up the confidence to move this way. Consider starting your client in a seated posture and then, as their comfort increases, gradually move to the hands-and-knees position or a full-body movement. Use the following scripts.

Sitting

1. *Start with either your right or left palm. Stretch the palm of that hand wide and spread the fingers wide. Now stretch the palm backward gently, as if you wanted to overextend your hand, until you feel a sensation in the center of your palm. Stretch until you feel the fascia in the inside of your palms stretch. It should be a pleasurable sensation.*

2. *Now do the other hand. Stretch the palm and fingers wide . . . and now stretch the palm backward gently until you feel the fascia stretch.*

3. *Alternate now between the two palms. The rhythm is stretch . . . release . . . stretch . . . release.*

4. *Repeat about five times and then notice the sensations in the palms of your hands.*

On Hands and Knees

1. *Come on to the floor on your hands and knees. You can support your knees with a blanket or mat for comfort.*

2. *Notice a neutral spine first. Center your chest and belly so it is neutral, not extended in either direction. Notice how your core muscles slightly engage when you do so.*

3. *Now gently curl your pelvis under and stretch your back as if you wanted to make a cat shape. Let your head curl under as well, as if you wanted to meet your tail with the crown of your head.*

4. *Feel the stretch in the whole back, following the pleasure sensation in the body. How does that feel?*

5. *Now switch direction and gently move toward a cow position. Gently arch the spine and let the head arch up, but don't overstretch it. Feel the stretch in the belly fascia now. The whole front of the body is stretching in both a passive and active way. Again, follow what feels good in the body.*

6. *Gently repeat these movements in a fluid and mindful way, each time finding more smooth transitions between the two postures. You are focusing in this practice on stretching the fascia, not a static yoga pose.*

Full-Body (Standing) Position

1. *Take a standing position, placing your feet wider than your hips.*

2. *Scan your body and where there is tightness, sensing into what wants to be pandiculated.*

3. *Begin to use a pandicular movement, starting with the hands, chest, and back.*

4. *Allow yourself to follow the stretch-and-contract movements that feel good in your body. Stretch what wants to be stretched . . . and contract. Work with this stretch-and-contract motion.*

5. *Follow the satisfaction of the pandicular movement, and let one motion follow another. Keep following the movement until you feel a "satisfactory" sensation in the body.*

REFLECTION

After the movement, have your client stand in open attention and notice the difference in their body and in their perceptions. Then invite them to complete the following prompts, either in writing or aloud with you:

- I feel . . .
- I sense in my body right now . . .
- The pandicular movement is . . .

Finding the Somatic Opening in the Body

PURPOSE

This tool teaches how to come into a relationship with the body as a friend and ally. This is an important tool when you offer any resourcing movement to your client. You want to look for the perceived somatic openings in the body. This can mean a calm place inside, a pleasurable sensation, a neutral feeling, a sensing place inside, or simply sensing the body without any activation and with curiosity. The intention is to explore an area of violation of the body that has gone numb, tight, or frozen with micro-movement and see if you can allow for somatic opening. Your client is working both on what has tightened up and how they can shift their awareness to include an opening.

INSTRUCTIONS

Guide your client through the following steps. Throughout the exercise, track for signs of ease and somatic opening—parasympathetic breath, gentle motion, soft emotion, long exhales, and so on—as well as signs of tightness, numbness, or frozenness in the body. Remember to go at the client's pace and with their consent to explore each opening and movement. Contact and somatically attune to what is arising in the process. Use the following script:

1. *In this movement exploration, I will ask you to open your attention to your body boundaries, times when these boundaries were crossed or violated, and how such a violation feels in your body. We will notice any somatic openings in the body, which are places where we can sense our body without activation and with curiosity. This might feel like a calm place inside, a pleasurable sensation, a neutral feeling, or simply a sensing place in the body. I want you to know that we will explore these somatic openings on your terms—we can slow down, pause, or stop whenever you like. We will go at the pace and in the direction that feels right for you. Would you like to begin?*

2. *First, identify a body boundary that you have or would like to have. This could be related to certain kinds of touch or movement, how others interact with your embodied self, or how you relate to and care for your own body. Describe this boundary. What is it? How does it protect or nourish you?*

3. *Slow down and go into mindfulness . . . get curious . . . and recall a time in your life when you experienced a crossing or violation of your body boundaries. This may be a memory of an uncomfortable touch or a time when you felt that your body was closed or withdrawn. Choose a memory that is workable for you, something that you feel comfortable exploring right now.*

4. *As you recall this memory, notice your body's response. Perhaps there is numbness, tightness, or a frozen or wooden feeling somewhere in your body. What do you notice? Where in your body do you notice this feeling?*

5. *Try to approach this place with curiosity and openness. Are you willing to explore this somatic opening?* [Track for signs of ease and somatic opening—e.g., parasympathetic breath, motion, emotion, exhales.]

6. *Going at your own pace, follow this somatic opening. Tune into this place in the body . . . how does this place feel?* [You can also ask the client to complete a prompt such as *"I now feel my _____ open," "What I feel is _____,"* or *"When I breathe, I can move with this tightness in my body, and I can also feel _____."*]

7. *Continue to notice this somatic opening with curiosity. What does it need? Would it like to move? You may wish to explore a micro-movement in or near this area. Slow down . . . notice . . . and follow this opening, this movement, wherever it needs to go.*

REFLECTION

Afterward, invite your client to answer the following questions in writing or aloud:

- What has changed and how?
- What is the somatic opening you're in touch with?

ROAMING Protocol

PURPOSE

You can teach your client how to get through moments of sympathetic nervous system activation with the ROAMING protocol. Practice this with your client when they are *not* triggered so they can remember and apply the protocol outside your office.

INSTRUCTIONS

Practice the protocol in steps; there are a lot to remember. Initially, you want the client to feel comfortable with the first four steps, such that the intensity of the trigger subsides and the client has a sense of being settled. Then you may continue with the remaining three steps.

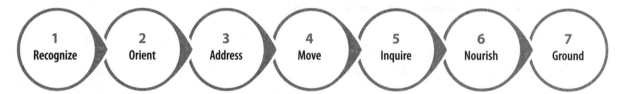

Talk your client through each step, using the following script as a guide:

1. **Recognize**

   - *Recognize you are being triggered.*
   - *Notice what is happening right now in your experience.*
   - *Become aware; acknowledge that you are triggered.*

2. **Orient**

   - *Look around the environment you are in.*
   - *Orient with your eyes physically in the space you are in. Follow your eyes—turn your head and look around.*
   - *Notice what is happening right now in your body. Take a baseline.*

3. **Address**

   - *Name what you are feeling in the present moment. Speak it out loud to yourself: "I am not there . . . I am here . . . with . . ." You are addressing the trigger directly.*
   - *Remind yourself: "The worst is over; I am experiencing a memory/sensation/emotion of the past. The past has arrived in the present. By being in the present, the past can leave now. Because I am safe now, I can be with the sensations and feelings that are coming up. Now is the time to honor my experience."*

4. **Move**

   - *Move! Move your body. You can stomp your feet or walk at a fast pace. You can push your arms out, or swing them. You can stand up and move your body in any way that feels supportive right now.*

   - *Using your breath and sound, make a sound like "pah" or " hah" as you forcefully exhale. You can use any sound that supports the moving breath.*

5. **Inquire**

   - *If the first four steps have settled you a bit, then you can do the next three. If you don't feel that settling, you might want to repeat steps 1–4 again.*

   - *Ask yourself, "Am I feeling and seeing myself?"*

6. **Nourish**

   - *Do one action that feels nourishing to you right now.*

   - *You might give yourself a hug or another kind self-touch.*

   - *Think of something that would nourish you right now.*

7. **Ground**

   - *Return back to baseline; ground yourself in the here and now.*

   - *Bring in a moment of gratitude for having gone through this trigger cycle.*

   - *Remember your body is your resource.*

   - *Remember all your relationships that are helpful and loving.*

   - *Ground yourself in the goodness of your life.*

REFLECTION

Invite your client into this reflection after they feel grounded again. This will help them remember that they know how to overcome the trigger cycle, so they can practice the steps when they are triggered in the future. They can discuss their responses with you or write them down.

- What was the initial trigger?

- What movement helped you?

- What nourished you?

- What are you grateful for?

- What do you want your future triggered self to know?

Protected and Safe

PURPOSE

Embodied safety is critical in establishing an inner sense of feeling protected from any outside attack. In this exercise, you are establishing a moving boundary of protection so your client can practice noticing when they don't feel safe and have a tool to reestablish the protection.

INSTRUCTIONS

Use the following script as a guide, and encourage your client to do this outside of session as needed:

1. *Imagine a big bubble around you. It can be any size, material, or color that you want. Take a moment to visualize this bubble all around your body.*

2. *Finish the following sentence: "My bubble around me is . . ."*

3. *Now add to your bubble a feeling of protection. It can be a quality that's strong, fierce, flexible, or whatever protective word comes to mind.*

4. *Finish the following sentence: "My bubble feels . . ."*

5. *Describe this bubble using your arms. You can use your hands and arms to start moving around the bubble as if you are drawing it in the air. Sense your way into this bubble all around your body. The bubble might change a bit or become something more concrete.*

6. *Finish the following sentence: "My bubble becomes . . ."*

7. *Now move your bubble in relation to the environment. Feel into what you need protection from. Think about times when you have felt threatened, when you could have found refuge in a safety zone.*

8. *Finish the following sentence: "I will use my bubble in times of _____ so I can establish my safety zone again."*

9. *Move in any way that will reinforce this sense of protection . . . then pause and notice your body.*

REFLECTION

Have your client write or draw how the bubble helps them feel protected and safe.

Grounding Movement: Making a Mark

PURPOSE

Introduce this movement as a reducing exercise, not a reenactment of a sympathetic charge. Feeling connected with the ground and one's weight on the ground is a quick and direct way to feel more resourced in the body. Here the focus is on connecting with safety.

INSTRUCTIONS

Use the following script as a guide. You may want to suggest to your client that they remove their shoes first.

1. *Stand upright and sense your baseline.*

2. *Notice what your connection with the ground is through your feet. Are your knees locked up? Are you feeling stiff or unbalanced?*

3. *Make any small adjustments through the body to loosen any stiffness or tightness in the body.*

4. *Now sense your feet and imagine they relate to the earth underneath. Notice the soles of your feet. Are they planted evenly? Are they lifted on the inside? Are the feet uneven on the ground? Is one foot heavier than the other?*

5. *Now lift one foot and leg up slightly. Hold it up for three seconds . . . and place it back down.*

6. *Lift the other foot for three seconds . . . and place it back down.*

7. *See if you can begin a rhythm of lifting and placing. Let the first round of lifting and placing be very light, as if you are simply arriving in the movement of placing the foot on the ground.*

8. *Notice the rhythm that begins inside. Is there a feeling that goes with it?*

9. *Repeat this rhythm and now add some weight to the placing of the foot, as if you are planting it deeper into the earth, making a mark. Imagine your foot is printing a small indentation on the ground.*

10. *Continue this rhythm and add as much or little weight as feels good to you. It might feel good to stomp and feel the whole weight of your body, or you might enjoy learning this footprint more slowly and gently.*

11. *Continue this until you feel a connection with the earth underneath you.*

12. *Pause and notice your body. What are the sensations in the feet, legs, and pelvis right now?*

13. *Complete the following statements:*
    - *"My body feels . . ."*
    - *"When I touch the ground, I am . . ."*
    - *"With my feet, I mark . . ."*

Rolling Gravity

PURPOSE

Feeling our connection with the ground is a stabilizing and resourcing experience. When we feel our relationship with gravity, we are sensing and feeling the body in deep, ancient connection. We are reminded that we have been away in attention and presence, and are finding our way back to ourselves. We often think that connecting with the ground needs to be static or held in a position. But grounding by moving in relation to the earth has a very different impact on your sense of connection. This exercise is a way to discover this.

INSTRUCTIONS

Prep your space so that your client can do this exercise lying on the floor. Consider in advance whether they will need some support beneath their back, head, or knees. Use this script as a guide:

1. *Find a comfortable spot on the floor and lie on your back.*

2. *Take a moment to sense the ground beneath you.*

3. *Tune into the earth underneath that is supporting you right now . . . as you exhale, you can give over any tension or weight you might be feeling.*

4. *When you notice that there is some calming and settling, bring your knees up, with your feet flat on the ground.*

5. *Begin by slowly moving the knees side to side, feeling a gentle twist in the waist. Make it a continuous movement.*

6. *Pay attention to the weight of your knees as they move sideways. Let your body follow the weight. Don't force anything; relax the movement and pace.*

7. *Gravity is your teacher here. Notice the weight of the knees and then let the body movement follow it. For example, you might notice your chest wants to start rolling in the same direction. Perhaps your head wants to come along or twist in the opposite direction. You are allowing gravity to guide the movement.*

8. *Bring the knees up again to the center of your body. Notice how they want to move toward the other side.*

9. *Make these movements in a mindful way so that you can sense into how the body begins to roll side to side . . . rolling side to side across the back, the knees being the initiator of the movement. Let that happen organically.*

10. *You are becoming a rolling, gentle see-saw . . . notice how the rest of the body rolls along with it.*

11. *Now tune your breath to this rhythm that is emerging . . . feel the joy and playfulness in this movement.*

12. *Do this until your body wants to come to a natural stopping.*

13. *Open your inner attention wide and notice the change in your body.*

14. *Now, complete the following sentences out loud:*

    - *"My body feels ..."*

    - *"Gravity teaches me that I am ..."*

    - *"My body in relation to the earth means ..."*

    - *"I am ..."*

Twirling Leaf

PURPOSE

This movement practice is designed to help your client regulate and calm themselves through movement and imagery. This exercise prepares them to enter into sensing their body and align with the organic movements of their body.

INSTRUCTIONS

Have you client be barefoot and standing for this exercise. Guide them through the following script:

1. *Lift the soles of your feet and wake up the feet by moving them gently around. Shift your weight around from side to side, from front to back . . . make the movements of your feet creative, unpredictable, random. Your aim is to wake up the sensations in the feet.*

2. *Plant your feet on the ground and notice what kind of connection you have from your feet to the ground. Do your calves and your legs feel more grounded too?*

3. *Now imagine that you are standing in nature close to a majestic tree. Allow yourself to see the details of this tree, ideally a wintry tree that has a few leaves left. They are about to drop from the tree.*

4. *As you watch a leaf fall, use one of your hands to mimic that movement of a leaf falling toward the ground. Let the journey of the leaf be slow and mindful.*

5. *Repeat this motion several times, following the journey of each leaf slowly falling to the ground.*

6. *What is the quality of this motion? What happens in your body as you move with this quality?*

7. *Pause for a moment. Is there a settling? How do you notice that right now?*

8. *Now refine the movement . . . repeat the movement quality . . . allow it to settle you until you feel complete.*

If you are doing this in a therapy session, ask your client about the quality that is now present and how it is different from where they started. Encourage discussion.

If you assign this exercise as a home practice, remind the client to reflect on what is available to them when they are settled. Ask them to do 10 minutes of writing, answering the following prompts:

- When I feel settled, I am . . .
- When I touch into the ground, I am . . .
- My internal sense of being settled is connected to . . .
- When I am settled and grounded, I imagine the tree being . . .
- The qualities of movement that are here now are . . .
- This is what tells me that I feel complete in myself . . .

Midline Motions

PURPOSE

This is a centering movement that you can offer if your client needs grounding. The midline is the center of the body. The term is a developmental reference, as a baby will cross their arms through the midline of their body as part of the growing nervous system and brain development. Consciously working with the midline is a fast and direct way to bring the client into a regulated state. You can use this motion both with highly activated states and with emotional frozen states. With the frozen state you want to offer imagery first, as bringing motion can be too big of a task; in this case, you can guide your client to imagine the center of their body, or picture a line down the front of their body they can trace with this motion.

TIPS

It is ideal to introduce this as a guided exercise. After practicing in session, encourage your client to do it anytime they feel unsettled or need to come back into their center.

INSTRUCTIONS

This exercise is ideally done standing. Your client should keep their eyes open initially. Once they are comfortable with the motion, they can close their eyes and sense the movement from the inside. Have them repeat this motion mindfully and to the moment when they notice a shift in their activation or a sense of becoming settled. Guide them through the following script:

1. *Find a solid stance when standing.*
2. *Become aware of your legs and feet; ground them into the floor. Keep your knees gently bent, so that you don't stiffen up the legs.*
3. *Let your arms hang loosely alongside your body.*
4. *Connect with your natural breath.*
5. *Take an inner baseline of how you are feeling at this moment. Name that out loud.*
6. *Imagine your body having a midline. You can imagine it like a thin line painted down the front of your body. It travels from the front of your forehead toward the end of your torso.*
7. *Now, slowly and deliberately raise your arms in synchrony sideways, stretching them out as you reach upward.*
8. *Turn your palms outward as you raise your arms.*
9. *Go slowly and bring the awareness of your breath with you.*

10. *Touch your hands above your head. If you can't reach them overhead or there is any stress reaching up high, just bring your hands together at the level of your forehead, face, or chest. Follow the range of motion that works for your body.*

11. *With your hands together above your head or wherever is comfortable, trace the midline down your forehead . . . face . . . neck . . . chest . . . belly . . . until your hands can't stay together anymore.*

12. *Let your arms rest alongside your body and notice. Name out loud what you are aware of.*

13. *Repeat this cycle three to five times, each time slowly raising, reaching, and then bringing together the hands to trace the midline of your body. Your thumbs are gently touching this imaginary line.*

14. *[After three to five cycles] Let your hands and arms rest. Notice and name what you are aware of now.*

15. *Sit down and have a moment of mindfulness to notice the change that has just occurred.*

Swaying

PURPOSE

This exercise uses swaying to settle activation. Swaying is an ancient motion found in many cultures. Mothers rock their children and sway their own bodies in order to soothe and settle. We sway with music or with the ocean waves. Swaying is an innate rhythm that our body likes to do when we feel the need to settle and soothe our nervous system.

TIPS

If your client is struggling with this practice, try playing music. You can also help them sway by mirroring this motion with them if that feels comfortable.

INSTRUCTIONS

This exercise is typically done standing, but it can easily be adapted for a sitting position or another preferred body posture. The swaying motion can be in the hands and arms or the torso alone. What matters is the rhythm and the attention to the quality of swaying. Track the frequency of the swaying motion and assess how it is soothing your client's nervous system. Guide them through this script:

1. *Sit or stand, and feel your feet on the ground.*

2. *Can you find a swaying movement right now? It can be a small, intrinsic movement or a hand motion to start. Feel into the rhythm of that swaying.*

3. *How is your breath responding?*

4. *Follow the rhythm that feels just right . . . notice how you are calming and settling. Find the rhythm that does just that.*

5. *[If mirroring seems wise, you can say:] I am doing that movement with you.*

6. *If it feels supportive, you can place a hand on your chest or belly and continue that swaying movement.*

7. *Notice if you are yawning or breathing more slowly.*

8. *Move until you find a natural stopping point.*

9. *Now let your attention go inward and be with the stillness, the calmness, that is here.*

10. *If this swaying motion could talk to you right now, what would it say?*

Psoas Muscle Release

PURPOSE

In this exercise you will help your client work with gentle and passive movements to release tension and holding deep in the psoas muscle. The psoas muscle plays a big role in holding trauma memories. It connects from the legs to the front of the spine. The psoas muscle is engaged when we are fleeing or fighting. It's part of our protective system and can create referred back pain and tightness in the groin.

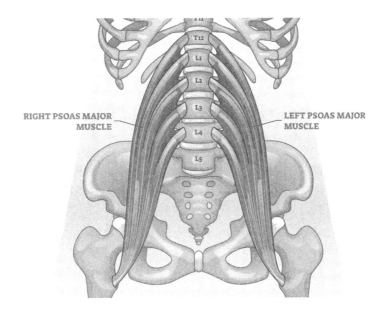

INSTRUCTIONS

This exercise requires a chair and space in front of it where the client can lie down. You will also want to have a small pillow and a blanket on hand so the client can support their head and lower back if needed. Use the following script as a guide:

1. *In this exercise, you will be using your breath and sensing into the psoas muscle, which is a kind of internal helper in challenging times. The psoas muscle connects from your legs to the front of your spine. It's part of your protective system; it engages when your body senses a threat that you may need to run away from or fight against. But this activation can lead to tension or pain, which is why befriending your psoas muscle helps to restore ease and relaxation.*

2. *Lay down on your back and rest your lower legs on the chair. Place your knees so they're touching the edges of the chair. You can use the blanket to cushion your lower back if needed, but aim for your back to be fairly flat on the ground. Support your head with the pillow. Let your arms rest on your body or alongside it.*

3. *Breathe into this posture first . . . notice how in this posture the body eases.*

4. *Let your knees relax and find the most comfortable position for a few minutes, breathing into the pelvis area at your own pace. Imagine that your psoas is your friend that has helped you through some tough situations by fleeing or fighting. Appreciate for a moment that this muscle has had the power to propel you to get away and carry you.*

5. *Let your knees come toward the center, and then let them gently fall to the side. Repeat that movement. Let your knees fall open and then bring them together in a smooth motion a few times.*

6. *Rest and breathe into the psoas region again. Notice any change.*

7. *Now slowly take one knee and bring it toward your chest, pulling it gently toward you and then extending the knee to the resting position again.*

8. *Switch and bring the other knee toward your chest, pulling it toward you and then resting.*

9. *Now coordinate this movement with your breath. As you bring your knee toward your chest, slowly exhale, and then mindfully inhale and rest your leg down on the chair again. Repeat this five to six times.*

10. *[After five to six repetitions] Now rest and scan your body . . . where do you feel the release?*

Moving Your Back Body

PURPOSE

This tool is for you to practice your own resource and return to it often. The back body is an essential somatic internal reference that can give you stabilizing capacities when working through challenging moments in session. While you can practice the back-body exercise in session, it is best done afterward. The intention is to return to your resource and reflect on how you hold on to the exchange and intensity of the work in your own soma. You can do this exercise sitting or lying down. The reflection prompts after the practice will help you to identify habitual somatic patterns.

INSTRUCTIONS

1. Take a seated meditation position and relax your body posture.

2. Take a few grounding breaths, connecting with your sitz bones.

3. Turn your attention to the whole back body, sitting relaxed but alert.

Back Body

4. Move your center of attention into the back body. Become aware of any kind of tension in your shoulders, chest, or back and begin a slow stretching movement toward the back body.

5. Move the back body into a gentle cat stretch as you exhale.

6. As you inhale, move the back into a neutral position.

7. Repeat this movement three times—stretching into the back, curving and exhaling, then moving the back into the center position while inhaling.

Side Body

8. Now move the back body to the right, as if you are stretching into your ribs sideways. Return to center.

9. Now move the back body to the left . . . stretch . . . and return to center.

10. Continue moving from side to center. Coordinate these movements with your exhale and inhale as it feels right in your body.

Rotating the Back-Body Positions

11. Now introduce a gentle rotating motion. Starting from the center, rotate your body to the right, back to the center, to the left, and back to the center again. Let that be one smooth, continuous movement and respect any limitation that might arise.

12. Pay attention to any kind of tension that your chest, belly, shoulders, and back are holding. As you move the whole barrel of your chest and belly in this way, become aware of how you may be holding any kind of emotional triggers from the previous session.

13. Repeat this movement until you feel a substantial shift within. Look for body indicators such as calming or a sense of spaciousness.

Rest and Reflect

14. Rest in the center of your body, feeling the back body without effort.

15. Turn toward the reflection questions and feel and sense into how you have been holding the session work in your own soma.

REFLECTION

Reflect on or journal about the following prompts:

- When I move my body, I can release my client's story in these ways: _____.

- When I work with my client, I hold their emotions of_____ in this part of my body: _____.

- When I work with my client, I hold their story of _____ in this part of my body: _____ or as this type of thought pattern: _____.

- When I work with my client, I notice I lose my connection with my resource of _____ by _____ [*name the pattern you identify when you lose connection*].

- My mind thinks I need to do _____ in the session, but my body feels _____.

- When I am moving my back body, I feel _____ and I know _____.

CHAPTER 8

SYMPATHETIC ACTION AND SELF-REGULATION

"The single client factor that best predicts success in psychotherapy is whether or not the client can 'stay' with his or her experience."

—**Ron Kurtz,** "Body Expression and Experience in Body Psychotherapy"

Our human nervous systems have been developing and adapting our responses to threats throughout evolutionary history. Our sympathetic nervous system developed 200 million years ago and equipped our bodies with the ability to fend for ourselves when there is a threat by running away or staying and fighting for our survival. These two active responses are key to understanding our mobility in therapeutic movement. Not only can we understand how our client had to act in protective ways, but we can also learn to see these fight and flight motions in the body as impulses. If we can learn to read these protective impulses, we can help the client to release and sequence toward the completion of these ancient survival movements.

Both fighting and fleeing are fast-action impulses. We want to move immediately and with speed to neutralize or remove ourselves from the perceived danger. This means that our body needs to prepare and act almost instantaneously to ensure the greatest chance of survival. After the amygdala sends a distress signal, the hypothalamus activates the sympathetic nervous system. The hypothalamus acts like a command center of the brain under stress. It stimulates the pituitary gland to release hormones into the adrenal glands, which secrete epinephrine and cortisol and drive the body into survival action. The adrenaline moves into the bloodstream, leading to a number of changes that prepare the body to respond to danger. The heart rate accelerates, pushing blood into the muscles and vital organs. Breathing becomes rapid as the lungs take in more oxygen to fuel mental focus on the threat. Nutrients are increased throughout the bloodstream to ensure enough energy for the following burst of activity.

This fight or flight response takes up vast energy in the body, enabling the person to act quickly, focusing on the survival task at hand. For a short period of time, the "gas pedal" of the sympathetic nervous system is activated. Typically, once the perceived threat has passed, the cortisol level will subside, dampening the stress response and allowing the person to return to a more relaxed state. However, chronic stress or trauma that has been stuck will result in these action systems not being processed to their full completion. The nervous system will continue to put out signals of danger, and the body can respond in micro-physical impulses, resulting in systemic problems over time (Smith & Vale, 2006).

Defensive Movements

Defensive movements are innate movements we utilize when we are under threat. They are survival movements of the body that act as protective responses to traumatic experiences. They include movements such as hunching, turning away, pushing away, kicking, clenching, making oneself small or big, and rigidity. While part of our survival toolkit, when chronically held and not consciously processed they can restrict full embodiment, emotional expression, and presence.

This can happen when the danger is too much or the defensive movement is overwhelmed, interrupted, or unsuccessful in its completion. The defensive movement can then become stuck in the body. Understanding the details of the defensive motion will help your client to complete any cut-off movements they might notice and become conscious of any associated feelings. Reconnecting with the actual defensive movements in safety and with mindfulness can help the client to regain control and a sense of self-agency in their body.

Defensive movements are part of our nervous system mobilization when we perceive danger, but they are also part of play and relational engagement that does not involve threat. For example, we use defensive motions to feel and set boundaries. As children we tussle and playfully learn where our physical boundaries are with others, how to embody strength and feel our own power.

Sequence Safe Defensive Movements

PURPOSE

The purpose of working with defensive movements is to make the unconscious conscious, so that your client develops a deeper connection with the inherently powerful defense system of their body. In this exercise, you will work with the following types of defensive movements: pushing, ducking, kicking, leaning in, twisting away, and jumping.

TIPS

Sequence awareness refers to paying attention to the whole movement, from beginning to end. With sequence awareness, we are aware of where a movement begins, follows through, and then impacts. For example, we tend to think of kicking as something we do with a foot, but when the client slows down and traces the full motion of their kick, they might notice it has an initial impulse in a muscle far from the foot, such as the hamstrings, hip adductors, or glutes. When you are guiding the client, you want to explore *how* the kick moves—its speed and quality, its pathway. Then, how does it feel when the kick lands? What is that impact? Ask the client: *Can you stay with the satisfaction and completion of this movement? Or do you pull backward even as you impact?* Make sure you track the entire sequence of defensive movements.

INSTRUCTIONS

You can work with defensive movements in therapy in two ways:

1. **Naturally, as part of their narrative:** Track for automatic defensive motions present in the client's expressions as part of their narrative. You might see pushing, bracing, fending off a hand, or other movements that support the spoken words in nonverbal narrative. As you read these movements, ask the client to slow down and simply notice how they are occurring.

2. **Intentionally:** Intentionally introduce defensive movements so that the client can become aware of how to mindfully reconnect with these primal motions.

   • Approach the defensive movements as a playful discovery process. This is not about getting the "right" movement; it's about having the client feel into and explore which motions make them feel in control and in power. Have the client try out different movements, pause frequently, and invite them to discover the meaning behind the movements. It's okay for the movements to be vigorous or fast, but establish some ground rules of safety for your client, yourself, and the physical space. If the movements become too intense, overwhelming, or confusing, bring mindful pauses and slow down the process. This might be the time to inquire about what is occurring emotionally. The aim is for the client to be fully with the sequence of the movement and feel its completion toward satisfaction.

- These six movements can be explored while standing or modified so the client can sit as needed. Practice sequence awareness (as described in the tips). Encourage mindful awareness as your client does these movements. Prompt them to notice changes in their breath, inner activation levels, sensations and feelings, and how they're exerting their physical body. Help them notice which movements give them joy or make them feel playful, satisfied, powerful, or challenged. Encourage them to notice how some movements may feel strange or unfamiliar, and to pay attention to the story that relates to that. You can ask your client, *Are there any defensive movements that are not accepted?*

Use the following scripts to guide your client through the different movements.

Push

1. *Start standing. With one foot, take a slight step forward for stability. Keep your knees bent slightly.*

2. *Stretch out your arms in front of you in a big push. Imagine you are pushing to make space, pushing something away from you.*

3. *Notice the exertion, notice the breath.*

4. *Where are you pushing from? Just the arms? Is the rest of the body connected?*

5. *What kind of body stance will make your push more powerful?*

6. *Now, fill in the blanks:*

   - *"I am pushing from _____."*

   - *"I am not engaging _____."*

   - *"I feel _____ when I push _____."*

Duck

1. *Start standing. Have your feet be light and mobile. What stance can help you be more agile?*

2. *Imagine now something coming at you that you want to evade.*

3. *Play with ducking the oncoming action toward you. You can explore being fast, sly, playful.*

4. *Pay attention as your body starts becoming more rhythmic. What image can support you being more agile?*

5. *Experiment with different kinds of ducking qualities. Feel the play in your body.*

6. *Now, fill in the blanks:*

   - *"When I duck, I feel _____."*

   - *"I can duck when I am _____."*

   - *"The movement of ducking reminds me of _____."*

Kick

For this movement, a pillow or other soft object can be useful.

1. *Start standing. Choose one standing leg that will support you doing a kick. Create a stable base before kicking.*

2. *With your kicking foot, begin with a flicker in your toes, as if you are wanting to lightly kick something out of the way.*

3. *Feel into the sensation as you engage the kicking motion. Notice your foot . . . your leg . . . involve your whole body.*

4. *If it's helpful, you can gently kick a pillow or another soft object. Notice the impact as you kick it. Can you connect with your body's movement and what that is evoking in you?*

5. *Now, fill in the blanks:*

   - *"When I kick, my body feels connected with _____."*
   - *"When I kick, I feel _____."*

Lean In

For this movement, you will need access to a wall or pillow.

1. *Start standing and ground your stance with both feet pressing into the floor. Make your body quite heavy and rooted.*

2. *Now lean your shoulder into a wall or pillow and add your weight to it. You can do this gradually or in small pushes.*

3. *Feel the weight and power in your body as you lean into the challenge. You might imagine that you are a large animal, such as a mighty bear or gorilla.*

4. *Feel your core muscles in the belly and notice from where you are leaning. What is more effective, leaning from the shoulder or the belly?*

5. *Ease up and notice your body before trying again. Make sure you use some weight, but also be mindful of the limitations of your body. You want to explore the movement and connect your power with this movement.*

6. *Now, fill in the blanks:*

   - *"When I lean in, I feel _____."*
   - *"Leaning makes me connect with _____."*
   - *"I imagine that I am a _____ when I lean my weight _____."*

Twist Away

1. *You can start standing or moving already. Imagine there are forces coming at you and you are twisting your body out of the way, avoiding being targeted.*

2. *Play with small twisting motions, rotating your waist or shoulders. Explore twisting out of the way with your hands, arms, feet, or whole body. Find what feels right. Make sure your body is safe and don't over-rotate your body into a twist that does not feel comfortable.*

3. *Play with being evasive and avoidant as a clever strategy to get away. Feel the joy and lightness that can come with this motion.*

4. *Now, fill in the blanks:*

   - *"When I twist away, I can _____."*

   - *"Once I am twisted away, I am able to _____."*

Jump

1. *Begin with a small jump. You can imagine jumping away from or toward something.*

2. *Notice as you jump how your body exerts force to lift up. Feel your heartbeat increase . . . notice how your body feels as you jump.*

3. *Do a few more jumps . . . and now become mindful. Pause and listen to your breath, your heartbeat, and the other sensations in your body.*

4. *What is the feeling that comes with jumping? Fill in the blank: "When I jump, I feel _____."*

REFLECTION

Take a moment and have your client reflect on the defensive movements they just explored. Ask them to answer the following questions, either aloud with you or in their journal:

- Which defensive movements are more common for you?

- Which ones are more unfamiliar?

- What came up for you as you explored these movements?

- Can you recognize that these are your innate ways of protecting yourself?

- What movement creates more safety for you?

Sequence the Flight Response

PURPOSE

This exercise will help your client learn to sequence a flight response in the body. Flight movements are part of protective impulses to evade danger. In the moment a threat is perceived, these movements often happen so quickly that the client may not even be aware of them. By doing the movements in a mindful and focused way, the client can learn to study the natural sequence in which a flight motion moves through the body. This deliberate action unlinks the stressful emotions and memory associations in the body. When your client can recognize movements in their body and the associated emotions, they have a much better chance when they are truly triggered to be able to discern more helpful response options.

INSTRUCTIONS

Have the client begin by setting an intention to explore the movement quality of flight. Because it can often be associated with fear or anxiety, you want to have the client pause frequently, go slow, and study the experience rather than amplifying it. Be sure to use sequence awareness (see the tips in the *Sequence Safe Defensive Movements* exercise).

You might explore the following flight movements:

- Impulse to run in the feet or toes
- Fidgety motions in the feet, legs, hands, or fingers
- Impulse in the front of the jaw
- Impulse in the chest to lean forward
- Bending, leaning, or twisting away with the torso, chest, or face
- Running or fast walking motions felt in the body or imagined

These flight movements can be explored standing or sitting. Start with a position that feels supportive to the client. You can work with flight movements as impulses felt in the feet, legs, hands, or torso. Say:

1. *Begin with the small impulses that want to "get away." Notice what your eyes are doing. Are they looking around? Are they vigilant, scanning the environment?*

2. *Pause and notice any tightness or speediness in the body. Take a few deep belly breaths and allow the body to settle.*

3. *Now come back to the impulse to flee and follow it mindfully.* [The client may get out of their chair, walk faster, or dart to a targeted place they have in mind. When they are done, continue.] *Pause*

and again notice your body. How did you do this in your body? What parts in your body mechanics
came to support you doing this quick action?

4. *Pause and settle back into a neutral place.*

5. *Now walk, or walk a bit faster, with the awareness that you are moving away. Feel the strength and*
   alignment in your walk. What supports this focused activity in your body? How does this movement
   of "away" feel to you right now? What is the sequence in this action of fleeing?

6. *Start walking a little bit slower . . . and even slower . . . until you come to a settled and calm place. Let*
   the walking come to a natural resting place.

7. *Say inside: "I successfully moved away. I am okay." Notice how that registers in your body.*

REFLECTION

Afterward, have your client write down or discuss their responses to the following prompts:

- My flight movement moves me away from _____.

- When I engage in this motion, I feel _____.

- What gets in the way to fully own this movement is _____.

- When I adjust my body in these ways: _____, I can do _____.

- When I move _____, my impact is _____.

- My sequence through the body is _____. [*Use metaphors or images that will help you remember*
  this sequence.]

- I will use my flight response when I am _____.

- The empowered quality about the flight movement for me now is _____.

- When I feel this flight movement impulse, the resourcing message I can give myself to settle this
  fleeing motion is _____.

- When I get triggered into the flight response in the future, I can give myself mental and somatic
  tips like these: _____.

Sequence the Fight Response

PURPOSE

This exercise shows how essential the fight response is as a defensive movement. The purpose is to help the client become in control of this movement and appreciate the benefit of this amazing resource in the body. They will learn to mindfully regulate and own the movement of defensive fight in their body, not act it out automatically. This exercise helps the client to embody the defensive response and understand it from the inside out. You also want to help your client connect to the positive aspect of this survival resource, not trigger any associated trauma, and to befriend the strength and intensity this defensive response can bring.

INSTRUCTIONS

This exercise needs to be guided so that you can help the client stay within their zone of tolerance and settle activations. The focus is on studying the movement as strength and inherent power. You want to avoid triggering the client; use your trauma-informed clinical judgment to assess the suitability of this tool for each specific client. Make sure you stay with sequence awareness (see the tips in the *Sequence Safe Defensive Movements* exercise) and gauge that the client is present with the movement. Look for where the client is more connected with themselves.

Pause frequently to encourage the client to study their internal experience; they will need their journal for this part. You want to teach your client how to consciously play with the movement, to embody the strength and the boundary that comes with it, without the emotional charge being overwhelming. Remind the client to feel the sequence of the fight response—where it begins, how it travels through the body, and where it ends. Make sure to track the client's breath and heart rate and encourage the client to slow down when needed. You want to work with the active charge in your client's body and then settle this charge back to a neutral zone. You will be able to study the effects of the sympathetic charge when the settling happens in their body more fully.

You might explore the following kinds of defensive fight movements:

- Pushing
- Punching
- Kicking
- Hammer punching
- Jabbing
- Flicking

Pick a movement that your client is curious about. Choose one that has some aliveness and playfulness to it. The first three movements—push, punch, and kick—are the classic movements we engage with when we need to fight. You can also explore some variations, such as a hammer punch (which involves having a closed fist and bringing the arm downward with force), a jabbing motion with one or two fingers, or a flicking motion with the tips of the fingers.

Guide your client through three cycles, and after each cycle have a settling period so the client can study their inner experience. If they feel too activated, please stop and work on settling and reestablishing a calm resource. You want to study the activation in their body in a constructive manner. If your client comes up against anger that begins to feel like too much, please have them pause, ground back into their feet and legs, and reflect. Then, either have them choose a different movement or grant them time to process. Throughout, remind your client to be gentle and kind with themselves. Explain that this exercise is about befriending a deep empowered movement in the body, not re-enacting. You can use the following script:

1. *This exercise is an exploration of your fight response—the defensive movements that happen when your body senses danger and a need to protect you by striking or forcing the threat away. This might involve pushing, punching, kicking, jabbing, or flicking motions. These movements can feel intense and even overwhelming, but we will explore them very mindfully and slowly, at whatever pace feels okay to you. By consciously engaging with these fight movements, slowing them down, and observing them with curiosity, you can come to better understand them. You may come to appreciate and befriend these movements as you see how their strength and intensity help to keep you safe.*

2. *Let's begin by setting an intention. What would you like to explore? For example, your intention might be "I want to understand and learn about my power to kick" or "I want to embody my power through feeling the strength of my pushing." Choose a fight movement that is not charged for you today. The goal is to learn about this movement, own it, and understand how it sequences in your body to completion.*

3. *As you are getting ready to explore, what do you notice in your body?* [If they're feeling nervous, anxious, or fluttery in the stomach, have them take a few breaths and slowly bring these activations into a neutral zone. Only then progress.]

4. *Stand with your feet solid on the floor, with one foot ahead of the other in a relaxed lunge position. Keep your knees slightly bent so your stance is mobile. Explore how you can be most solid in this standing position.*

First Cycle

5. *Explore the motion you chose.* [Have them complete the motion at whatever speed initially comes to them.]

6. *Now pause and notice your inner experience. In your journal, write down your responses to the following questions:*

   - *As you did this defensive movement, what happened to your breath? To your heart rate?*
   - *What did you see inside as you engaged with that movement?*

7. [Wait until their body is settled and their breathing is neutral before doing the second cycle.]

Second Cycle

8. *Repeat that movement—but this time, slow it down, as if it's in slow motion. Really be with each of the mini-motions that make up the larger movement; notice how this movement sequences through your body. Get curious about this sequence.*

9. [When they reach the impact moment] *Hold here. What experience arises for you?*

10. *Come back to a neutral position . . . allow your body to settle and relax.*

11. *Write down your responses to the following questions:*

    - *What is the impact of your defensive movement?*
    - *Where do you feel that original impulse in your body?*
    - *Where does the movement want to travel toward?*
    - *What happens as you complete the movement?*

12. [Once the client is settled, continue with the third cycle.]

Third Cycle

13. *Now you will do the same movement and go for the actual impact, bringing along the knowledge you've just gained about the sequence. This might be fast and with some force to it. You can use your exhale breath or a sound as you do this movement. Follow the movement through to its impact now.*

14. *Pause and study the activation in your body right now. Write down your responses to the following questions:*

    - *How is the activation in your body different?*
    - *What are the nuances you may not have noticed before?*
    - *What is intelligent about this movement?*

15. [You might need to ask your client to repeat the second and third cycles to fully understand the movement sequence. Feel free to do so, but make sure that you follow these by resetting and pausing.]

REFLECTION

After completing the three cycles, have your client pause again and write down their responses to these prompts:

- My intention was _____.
- In the first cycle, I learned _____.
- I settled and saw _____.
- In the second cycle, I learned _____.
- I settled and felt _____.
- In the third cycle, I learned _____.
- I settled and knew _____.
- My fight position is _____.
- When I engage in this motion, I feel _____.
- What gets in the way to fully own this movement is _____.
- When I adjust my body in these ways: _____, I can do _____.
- When I move _____, my impact is _____.
- My sequence through the body is _____. [*Have them use metaphors or images that will help them remember this sequence.*]
- I will use my fight response when I am _____.
- The empowered quality about the defensive fight movement for me now is _____.
- When I feel this fight movement impulse in the future, I can remind myself to stay present with its intentions and wisdom in my body by saying _____.

Slow Push and Defend with Core Awareness

PURPOSE

You can use this practice when you notice impulses in the client's arms connected to pushing or defending motions. Notice where the motion stops or get stuck. Pushing motions may occur when there is high activation in the client's body or can be consciously applied when there is a feeling of low energy. The purpose is to help the client gain control of the pushing movement and feel the satisfaction of a defensive action.

TIPS

Track for signs of overwhelm; when you notice this, stop and have the client re-center before proceeding. The more mindfulness you can bring to this practice, the more the client will work on restoring their sense of control. You want to make sure the client can be with this motion without being overwhelmed by their anger. The slower and more deliberately you go, the better. Avoid fast acting-out motions that will activate the client further.

INSTRUCTIONS

When you notice the client having an impulse to make a pushing or defending motion while they are recalling their narrative, you can say, "I noticed you did this motion." Mirror the movement for the client and ask if they are interested in exploring it. If not, let it go. If they are, you can proceed with the following script as a guide. The client can do this motion standing or sitting down.

1. *Let's get curious about this movement. Where and how do you feel your center or core right now?*

2. *Begin moving your arms up from your core, very slowly. As you slowly lift your arms, stay connected with your core. If you lose that connection, back up and slow down even more to really feel that connection.*

3. *Keep lifting your arms and create a motion to push. You can imagine an object that you are moving or simply feel the action of your body moving.*

4. *Keep being connected with your core as you form the pushing motion forward at the height of your chest.*

5. *Bring your arms back as if you are drawing them inward toward your shoulders . . . and now push them back out.*

6. *Exhale as you push and let the inhale come naturally.*

7. *Slowly repeat this pushing motion a few times until you really feel the connection with your core and the power of your arms.* [Track carefully when there are feelings of dissociation or collapse

happening. Pause here and notice. Resource at that moment. The aim is to have the client feel the connection to pushing, boundaries, and healthy anger that is empowering.] *Go ahead if there is a word or sound that goes with that motion.*

8. [After five to seven repetitions] *Now, slowly bring down your arms and rest them. Notice the heightened sensations of your body.*

REFLECTION

Ask the client to respond to the following prompts out loud or in their journal:

- What did you notice during this exploration?
- Did you feel a sense of power?
- What feels protective about this movement?
- What is happening with your connection to your core right now?
- As you feel your body now, what message is here from your body?

Safe Flight Movements

PURPOSE

In this exercise you are helping your client to mindfully explore the impulse and movements of protective fleeing. The goal is for the client to stay with the actual movement, let go of the narrative, and allow their body to feel the freedom and play of the running impulse.

INSTRUCTIONS

This exercise can be done sitting or standing. It is best for the client to have no shoes on and to have firm contact with the floor. Say:

1. *Stand or sit and feel your feet flat on the floor. Now, start dragging one foot across the floor in a wiping motion.*

2. *At the end of the wiping motion, pick the foot up and place it on the ground with some weight.*

3. *Drag-lift-thump is the rhythm. Repeat this movement on one side about five times . . . and now switch sides. The dragging motion is meant to give you the sensation of moving the ground or surface beneath you, or you might feel as if you are moving in place.*

4. *Next, start with the same drag-lift-thump motion and then notice whether you have an impulse to actually move farther. Experiment with whatever movements spontaneously come up. You might have an image of running or want to walk and run. See if you can follow that impulse. Allow it to be there. You also might feel perfectly fine to stay with this dragging motion and feel the sensation of fleeing. Feel the ground beneath you as it creates stability for you to explore the possibility of flight movement.*

5. *Now slow down and study your experience:*

   - *What is available in your awareness now?*
   - *What happens when you are successfully fleeing?*
   - *What opens in your body when you flee?*
   - *What words come to you as you feel your body now?*

Brushing and Moving

PURPOSE

This exercise is helpful when there is agitation in the client's body that is difficult to settle or soothe and mindfulness may be difficult for them to practice. The fast-moving pace helps to meet the higher activation in the body and move it through. You want this high charge to move and settle, so your client will not move for too long, only until the intensity has moved on. You want to guide your client and carefully observe that they can be with this movement and then release and settle.

INSTRUCTIONS

Guide your client through the following script:

1. *Take a wide stance and ground your feet into the earth.*

2. *Start with your right hand and brush it down your left arm, from shoulder to wrist, in a fast motion, as if you are wiping something off your arm.*

3. *Now switch to the other side. With your left hand, starting from the top of your right shoulder, brush downward to your wrist.*

4. *Switch back and forth between brushing one arm and then the other, while you add some side-to-side movement to the whole body.*

5. *Let this become a rhythmic activity. It can be helpful to add some strong, short bursts of exhales or a sound such as "Swoosh!" or "Hah!"*

6. *Pause and see if you need to continue the movement. If the intensity has moved through, stop the movement and let your body naturally settle. You can take a seat or lie down on the floor and let your body come to a resting place on its own.*

Moving Through Intensity

PURPOSE

This exercise is for the moments in session when there is a highly activated state. When you see the client getting stuck in emotionally high-charged states or experiencing body agitation without words, you can encourage the client to move their body. Sometimes the emotional intensity needs to be met with movements that are quick, fast-paced, erratic, or chaotic. These movements are gateways into the inner resources of your client's body when you are able to meet and guide the client. Make sure you encourage the body to "move with it" and "breathe with it"; eventually the movements will synchronize and begin to settle on their own pace. This is a good moment to move and mirror your client's movement if there is enough therapeutic safety.

INSTRUCTIONS

Your focus will be to track this activation journey and name each movement to help the client to connect with it. Highlight how their marvelous body will guide them right through the intensity, with your help. Then you will safely scaffold your client back into a tolerable zone of activation. Read this script in a calm and steady voice. Make sure you're grounded and not activated yourself.

1. *There is a lot of energy or activation here right now. Let's move through this right now. I am here with you.*

2. *I am noticing that your _____ [body part and movement—for example, right foot is twitching]. Go ahead and follow that movement.*

3. *As you move in this way, bring some breaths with you . . . I see that you are moving. Let the body move, just move it, just move . . .*

4. *It will be okay. Your body is trustworthy. Let's follow what is emerging here right now.*

5. *Go ahead and move . . . you can slow it down or make it faster . . . let the intensity move right through you. Nothing lasts . . . move . . . just trust that movement . . .*

6. [Track for deeper breaths, or a slowing down of the intensity, and then meet that slowed pace.] *Notice how you are taking a deeper breath . . . there are some feelings that are coming along with it. Allow that too. Let that be part of the movement.*

7. *See if you can notice what wants to happen next . . . it seems to slow down a bit, huh?* [As you scaffold the intensity toward a more regulated state, follow this in the client. You want to point out how their body is settling and how they are doing well just moving right through the intensity without overwhelm.]

8. *Let's rest and pause. See if you can tune into the slowed rhythm of your breath. Let the movements be smaller . . . let them come to a natural settling place.*

REFLECTION

Ask the client to respond to the following prompts out loud or in their journal:

- What is the intelligence of intense movements?
- How do they serve you?
- What are these qualities expressing for you?
- What is behind the intensity?

Write and Move It!

PURPOSE

This technique is a powerful tool to move high-energy states and introduce writing techniques alongside it. You will need paper and writing utensils. This is not journal writing but writing words and phrases that get elicited while moving. Encourage the client to go back and forth between moving the body and writing, transitioning fluidly between the mediums. This will facilitate the expression of the hyperactivation into self-regulation through self-reflection.

TIPS

Think of the written words as movement, not as needing to make sense. Creating meaning will arise after the process.

INSTRUCTIONS

Your focus is to encourage movement on and off the paper. This will help modulate the arousal level within the client as well as open the process to more inquiry. You want to include mindful breathing, inviting them to slow down and sense themselves in the movement as well as on the paper.

1. Set up the room with at least three pieces of paper and lots of markers on the floor in front of the client. Let them know that this is an interactive process between the moving body in space and the moving body on paper.

2. Invite your client into this process by suggesting: *Let's try moving this intense or high energy through your body, and then you will continue this motion on the paper.*

3. Encourage your client to move their body in response to what they are sensing right now: *Allow your body to move in any way that feels aligned to where you are at. Go ahead and use your breath and all the body parts that want to be included.* They can be sitting, standing, lying down, or wherever else they want to start. They can change their body posture at any time.

4. After a few minutes of moving, invite the client to write and scribble. Let a word, letter, or phrase emerge. It can be small or fill the whole page. There are no limitations. You can say, *Feel the movement of the pen* as *motion. Don't think, analyze, or make meaning. This is a process of unfolding; trust it.*

5. After the client has finished writing, say, *Now move your body without writing. You can change your posture. See what feels right now. What movements want to happen now?*

6. After a few minutes of the new movement, invite writing again. This time, have your client notice what is coming through. It could be more phrases, a story, word salad. Have them write it all down. Remind your client to write *as* movement. Let the creativity be there.

7. Invite the client to do one more movement cycle and let it be an integrative one. You can ask, *What are the qualities of your movement now? What has shifted? What is happening now in your body? What has become clear? What are the words and movements that belong together and make sense? What is a mystery and not known? What are you curious about?*

REFLECTION

After their body has settled, talk with your client about their insights and reflections. Invite them to go over their writing and see what elements stand out, whether it is because they are new, familiar, or simply have a truth to them. You can do the same. A helpful technique is to highlight the words that stand out, then ask your client to integrate what they have learned. If help is needed, you can point out somatic openings that you noticed. Ask, *What has changed? What has been moved through?*

Movement Protocol for Nightmares and Flashbacks

PURPOSE

This protocol can be used as a mindful moving ritual before sleep to help prevent nightmares. It can also be used when you wake up during the night or anytime you have a flashback. It's designed to interrupt the fear cycle and to shift the intensity out of that moment.

INSTRUCTIONS

Before you try this exercise at home, it's important to discuss the steps with your therapist and do a practice run in the office together. This will allow you to explore the kinds of movements that will be helpful. In addition, it gives you the opportunity to discuss what images of compassion and resource will be useful to call upon when needed.

When practicing the protocol on your own, you can use the journaling part of the exercise and the *Tracking Nightmares and Flashbacks* tool that follows to note what you might like to discuss with your therapist and to track the progress you make.

Be patient and kind with yourself. Orient to the present moment.

Before Sleep: Set Your Conscious Intention

1. Set an intention for the night. For example: "Tonight I will be able to rest. If I wake, I will move through my fearful nightmares by moving my body."

2. Bring to mind a safe space—this might be a feeling of safety in your body, a particular spot in your physical home, a place in nature that you love, or a place that you create with your imagination. Breathe slowly into that place of safety and say, "I am safe now and I will be safe."

3. Quiet your mind and body before going to bed. You might stretch, do yoga, or read a calming book. Consciously slow down.

4. Remember your inner compassionate witnessing part. You can tell yourself, "When I wake, I will be able to notice my experience. I will be able to be kind and compassionate with myself. I have tools to work with my fears."

5. Call forth a resource in your life. This might be a loving person, a natural place, or any other resource that reminds you of safety and goodness in your life. Ask this resource to be with you when you wake at night. It can be helpful to have a physical reminder, such as a rock, a photo, or a beloved object you will look at or hold when you wake up.

Before Sleep: Journaling

1. In your journal, copy the following sentences and fill in the blanks. This practice is designed to "empty out" your worries.

   - Today I have been really scared of _____ [*simply name it, no details*].

   - I might have a nightmare and wake up feeling _____ [*name the emotion, usually fear*].

   - And my heart might beat fast, and I might be shaking or crying.

   - If that happens, I will tell myself it is because I am remembering _____ [*name it again, no details*].

   - Then I will turn on the light and orient around at my room. I will notice my space and what I see.

   - I will tell myself: "I just had a nightmare/flashback. This _____ [*event*] is in the past and not happening now."

   - I will remember my resource of _____ [*person, place, etc. that offers support and safety*].

   - I know that I can overcome this fear of _____.

   - I will move my body. Even if I feel fearful and frozen, I commit to moving my body now.

In the Moment: Moving

1. When you wake up from a nightmare or have a flashback, remind yourself of where you are now. Say out loud, "I am here in _____ [*location*]. It is _____ [*day and time*]. I am in the present. I am not in the past event. The past is behind me; it is no longer here."

2. Engage in a calm breathing cycle. Slowly inhale to the count of 5 and exhale to the count of 8. Slow down as much as you can.

3. Begin to bring body awareness through moving your body. Simply move in whatever way feels supportive, even slowly or just a little bit. Moving is critical in interrupting the fear cycle.

Right After the Moment: Regulation

1. As you regulate, recall your resource so you can stay anchored in the practice. Use the physical object or image if you have one.

2. Allow for sufficient time to orient, see, hear, and reassure yourself that there is no active danger in this moment.

3. Notice how quiet or calm you are after this protocol.

4. Thank your body for moving with you as a companion to move through the fearful place.

Afterward: Follow Up in the Morning

1. Reflect on what happened last night by appreciating how you were able to regulate yourself. This is a moment to be celebrating your follow-through. Well done!

2. Reflect on how moving your body helped you. What kind of movements worked for you? Note them.

3. Sit quietly and reflect on how you are overcoming the "inner terrors" one step at a time by emphasizing your strength and capacity to deal with the situation. You can say, "I was able to meet my inner terror by _____."

4. Remind yourself: "I am on my unique healing path. My tools are _____."

5. Journal or draw your experience. Focus on how you worked with it and the changes you have been experiencing.

6. If judgment, dismissive feelings, or criticism come up, make them visible by naming them. Remember that these feelings are here trying to help you process.

   - "My critic says _____."
   - "My judgments are _____."
   - "I want to dismiss _____."
   - "I remind myself of my goal to _____."
   - "When I move with my critical, judgmental, or dismissive parts, they are trying to help me with _____."
   - "If the part of me that is a critic could have a movement expression and a feeling, it would be _____ [*name the quality, energy, animal, etc. that externalizes the judgment or critic*]."

7. Practice a moment of gratitude. Healing trauma is hard work.

Tracking Nightmares and Flashbacks

Use this template to record your progress on your sleep and experience with the *Movement Protocol for Nightmares and Flashbacks*.

MOVE!	What prep activity before sleeping did you do?	What time and how often did you wake?	What movement or breathwork did you do?	What helped most?	Were you able to go back to sleep and rest?	How did you feel the next day?
Monday						
Tuesday						
Wednesday						
Thursday						
Friday						

Saturday	
Sunday	

REFLECTION

1. What kind of movements did you notice your body likes to do before bedtime?

_____

_____

2. How did you get through the flashback or nightmare? What did you notice in your body?

_____

_____

3. What can you change or strengthen in your nighttime routine to help you rest better?

_____

_____

CHAPTER 9

SELF–REGULATION WITH THE PARASYMPATHETIC CONTINUUM

"We should notice that we are already supported every moment. There is the earth below our feet and there is the air, filling our lungs and emptying them. We should begin from this when we need support."

—**Natalie Goldberg,** *Writing Down the Bones*

Befriending the Parasympathetic Continuum

The parasympathetic autonomic nervous system has two branches: *ventral vagal* and *dorsal vagal*. The "rest and digest" capacity of the ventral vagal complex allows the body to settle and relax after activation. It also gives us the ability to be creative and to engage with others. This ventral vagal complex helps us to restore our sense of embodied safety and connection with self and others. It is essential in healing trauma to learn to regulate back into the rest and digest mode.

The other part of the parasympathetic nervous system, the dorsal vagal complex, enables a shutdown state. When we are frightened or feel a threat to our safety, we can emotionally and physically freeze. This freeze or immobility response is often associated with complex relational trauma and can occur when processing trauma memories. This type of response has several stages or variations, from a momentary emotional freeze in the face of a socially perceived threat to a full-on fawning and submit response when there is a threat to one's life and bodily safety. The nervous system perception of threat is individual and can be triggered when not expected. Part of somatic trauma therapy is to learn about one's own autonomic nervous system function and how to engage with it.

There are four trauma responses in total: flight, fight, freeze, and fawn. These can also show up as hybrid states. The freeze response can feel to the client as wanting to withdraw. In the body, the freeze response is a non-movement that is held on the outside, to avoid more danger; the outer stillness of the body is presumed to prevent a predator from causing harm. This non-movement is only designed for a temporary situation; once the danger is over, we need to release the freeze and process it. If the freeze response gets stuck and is not released, the client can become a chronic non-mover and the interrupted response will continue triggering associated beliefs and nervous system responses. It becomes a vigilant and anticipatory impulse of expecting to freeze at any moment.

If the client can understand the freeze as a psychological and somatic response to a threat, they can also understand that it will not last. There is movement underneath the freeze; it's just not visible or consciously felt yet. But they can learn to befriend this non-movement and notice the movement that is still there deep inside their body. Often it will be perceived in a small breath motion or a tingling sensation in a part of the body.

The following chart can help you identify the stages to track when the client gets activated, so you can offer interventions to prevent the client from repeating the shutdown response. Tracking the early signs of the freeze response can be very helpful for the client to learn about their body.

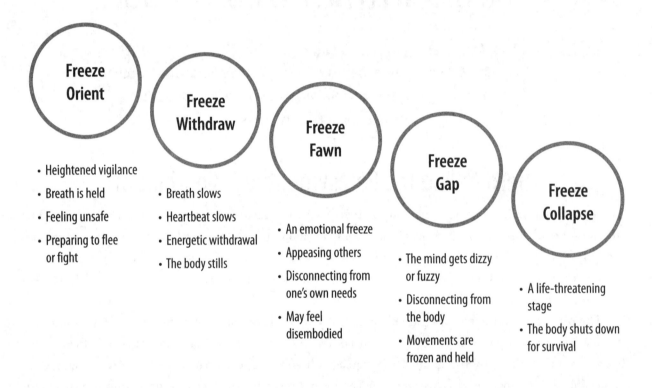

FREEZE MOVEMENT CONTINUUM

Freeze Orient
- Heightened vigilance
- Breath is held
- Feeling unsafe
- Preparing to flee or fight

Freeze Withdraw
- Breath slows
- Heartbeat slows
- Energetic withdrawal
- The body stills

Freeze Fawn
- An emotional freeze
- Appeasing others
- Disconnecting from one's own needs
- May feel disembodied

Freeze Gap
- The mind gets dizzy or fuzzy
- Disconnecting from the body
- Movements are frozen and held

Freeze Collapse
- A life-threatening stage
- The body shuts down for survival

Accessing Techniques

Often, memories of running, fighting, freezing, and appeasing are held in movement patterns beyond cognition. Movement explorations allow the client to touch into the nonverbal experience of trauma and how the body has either moved through it, gotten stuck, or created a habitual pattern to cope. You want to be mindful to learn about *how* the client is moving. This is not about goal-orientation; it's a study of patterns and the pathway of releasing any activation safely through innate somatic intelligence. You can use *accessing techniques* to help the client to stay and explore the movements.

Accessing is a way to resource and safely work with deeper trauma material that is held in the doing body. *Accessing questions* engage the curious inner wandering of the mover to discover what is next or wants to unfold. The movement becomes an access tool to a deeper embodiment and discovery of a theme or a memory. Accessing questions open a pathway toward enlisting an inner witness and healing intelligence.

Accessing directives steer the client to pause and go deeper with the experience they are having. You are encouraging the client to not be afraid of the experience and the movement currently. You are helping them to ally with the part of themselves that wants to be known and soothe the other, more fearful or shameful parts that don't know how to recognize the movement. See the exercise *Accessing Through Movement* for directions.

Boundaries

Boundaries are an essential practice in trauma healing. Many trauma experiences involve a physical, energetic, or emotional boundary violation. Often, this occurs within close relationships with people in positions of authority. When the client learns to understand where and how their boundaries have been breached, they also get details about how to learn to set boundaries. Many trauma clients report that it's difficult to know what a boundary is or how to set one. This is where exercises like *Boundary Movement* can be helpful.

Another useful exercise is the *Halt Hand Boundary*, which has origins going back to the uterus. Indeed, a fetus has the capacity to reflexively do the halt motion to fend off an intrusion. The fetus is not conscious of the action but will use the hand to defend itself (Sparling et al., 1999). This is part of the early reflexes in the developing body that later become defensive and conscious movements. At week 12 the fetus can feel pain, as the spinal nerves that connect information from the thalamus to the spinal cord have been developed. Movements like the halt hand develop in utero as impulses and nervous system responses to stimuli and are the early templates of how we communicate ex utero boundaries.

Recognizing the Freeze Movement Continuum

PURPOSE

This is a reflective exercise and movement exploration that you can practice with your client to help them identify and befriend the freeze response. You will help your client work with the first four freeze continuum responses and befriend the *no* in the body.

INSTRUCTIONS

Use the following script to guide your client:

The freeze response is a non-movement to avoid more danger. It's meant to be temporary, but sometimes we can get stuck in it. In this case, we need to befriend the non-movement with a movement so we can become unstuck.

I will describe different stages of the freeze response, and as I do, I invite you to explore how it feels to mindfully experience each stage. You might recall a moment in your life when you felt that way or simply imagine how it would feel to experience it.

Freeze Orient

*In the **freeze orient** stage of the response, you are assessing the level of threat that you detected. Your awareness is very heightened; your whole body becomes vigilant, readying itself to spring into action or to freeze further. The breath can be temporarily held. The senses are very tuned and alert. Your focus is sharp and concentrated. You are trying to orient into where you are and what needs to happen. Here's what I want you to do in this stage:*

1. *Appreciate your alert state.*

2. *Move your eyes and head and look around with intention.*

3. *Say inside: "I am checking for safety."*

4. *Notice any movements that your body wants to do now. This can be a small motion, a hand movement, a deeper breath, a sound . . . let that be. You can simply notice the impulse. Where does it start?*

Freeze Withdraw

*If the threat level persists, you will likely move into the **freeze withdraw** stage of the freeze response. Your breath slows, your heartbeat slows, and your energy withdraws. Your body becomes still. Here's what I want you to do in this stage:*

1. *Accept that your body needs to start protecting you.*

2. *Connect with the breath inside; feel the movement of the breath as movement.*

3. *Say inside: "I am protecting myself and can stay connected with myself."*

4. *Do you notice any movements that your body wants to do now?*

Freeze Fawn

*The next stage of the freeze response is known as **freeze fawn**. In this stage, you want to please or appease others and you disconnect from your own needs. You might start to feel disconnected from your body as well. Here's what I want you to do in this stage:*

1. *Befriend this smart part of yours that knows how to stay safe by fawning and pleasing others.*

2. *Connect with your capacity to track others as a relational intelligence.*

3. *Say inside: "I am staying safe and hidden, and I can return to myself."*

4. *Do you notice any movements that your body wants to do now?*

Freeze Gap

*In the next stage of the freeze response, called the **freeze gap**, the mind gets dizzy or fuzzy. You feel as if you are disconnecting from your body. Here's what I want you to do in this stage:*

1. *Bring some compassion to this situation. You might remember a person or spiritual figure that has unconditional regard for you.*

2. *Accept the fuzzy, disconnected feeling and know that this does not last.*

3. *Say inside: "It's okay. I will be okay. Clarity and connection will return."*

4. *Do you notice any movements that your body wants to do now?*

REFLECTION

Have your client journal about their experience with this protocol.

Unfurling to Unfold

PURPOSE

The purpose of this exercise is to bring a sense of fluidity and ease into the body. There are two moments when you can use this movement. One opportunity is when you observe a curling in of the head or chest and a quality of stuckness in the client's posture. Another opportunity is when the client describes or you notice a frozenness in the spine or stiffness in their posture. In either case, you can suggest this movement to allow a gentle flow and resource the curling-in motion.

INSTRUCTIONS

This can be done sitting or standing. Guide your client through this script:

1. *Allow yourself to curl forward until you find a stopping place.*

2. *Now see if you can create an unfurling motion. You can think of a fern unfurling, or a gentle wave ebbing and flowing . . . allow a movement of unfurling upward. Make sure you don't overextend the spine; just slowly roll up.*

3. *Now roll down the spine with one fluid motion. Let that be a gentle movement. Find the smoothness in that motion. Take your time. Notice the breath slowing down as you unfurl.*

REFLECTION

Ask the client to write down what they experienced. They can also answer, *What image goes with the unfurling for you?*

Accessing Through Movement

PURPOSE

Use accessing techniques to resource and safely access deeper trauma material that is held in the body. Without your guidance, the client might not be encouraged to explore what is new or challenging.

INSTRUCTIONS

1. Make sure your voice is kind, gentle, and inviting throughout. Invite the client to start. Ask them if they have a memory or theme they are working on. If it's a concrete trauma memory, make sure you resource first, go slowly, and pause whenever the client feels overwhelmed. The movement should be in support of the trauma memory moving *through* the body safely and with control. It's *not* a reenactment!

2. Say: *Start with a movement that feels centering, or grounding, or fluid, or simply pleasant.*

3. *Describe the feeling that goes with this movement. Where in your body does this movement and feeling reside?* [Anchor it by mirroring the client's movement or reflecting back what you heard.]

4. *Pause for a moment and notice the effect of the centering. Simply be aware and notice . . . know that you can come to this centered place at any time.*

5. *Now think of what you want to work on—the memory, feeling, or theme you want to explore. Name it out loud.* [This should be a short description; do not get into discussion.]

6. *What movement goes with this experience that you are exploring? Allow yourself to follow this movement.*

7. Use accessing questions to see where and how they are relating to the trauma material:

   - *What kind of resource quality is in this movement right now?*

   - *Where does the movement want to lead you?*

   - *How can you slow down this motion?*

   - *If this movement had a* [stronger, softer, etc.] *quality, what would that be right now?*

   - *Can you notice how the whole body is moving along with this emotion?*

8. Gently use accessing directives to encourage the client to stay and study the experience through movement. Let the experience unfold. If there are emotions that are moving with the body, allow that and be supportive. Say:

   - *Go ahead and move with this resource you are sensing in your body right now. Take your time and allow this movement to unfold in whatever way it wants. See if you can just be with this quality that is coming through.*

   - *Get curious about the rhythm and intensity of this motion.*

   - *Stay with that movement.*

   - *Discover what wants to happen next.*

   - *Let yourself really study this* [delicate, gentle, etc.] *motion. Allow the movement just as it is.*

9. If there is overwhelm or a freeze, then you can offer the resourcing movement. However, don't assume a freeze always needs to be resourced. If there is safety and trust in the movement process, the client will often want to explore the freeze as a micro-motion. Guide them; stay with that tiny freeze motion; go ahead and explore. Remember: There is always movement, even in a freeze!

10. Have the client keep moving, however small the movement needs to be. This is critical. The message to the body is that we touch the memory in the body and we are also connecting with something bigger. It can be self-compassion, feeling an emotion, a piece of memory that wasn't realized, sensations that weren't felt before, or anything else. Be patient and encourage the completion of the movement.

11. Take notes on the following:

    - What kinds of movements are showing up in the client's body, and for how long?

    - What supports the movements?

    - What interrupts the movements?

    - Where in the body are the moving resources?

    - What patterns of motion do you track?

12. Let the client rest. Debrief and have the client bring the experience into cognitive understanding. Have them reflect on these questions:

    - Where did the freeze movement open in your body?

    - What movement was most helpful to you?

    - What movement showed you that there was more than the freeze in your body?

    - What is the feeling in your body now?

One Cycle at a Time—Moving Feet

PURPOSE

This exercise will help to process somatic memories. Especially when there is an overwhelming or flooding feeling, this focused movement will help to settle the client's body. You can use this to regulate down or to help process tightness or a trauma memory in the body. You will be working on one feeling and one cycle at a time. This will help the client to gain a sense of control and self-agency in their body. It will help settle nervous system activation by engaging the fascia (see chapter 7) in the feet. This exercise can be followed with *One Cycle at a Time—Cross-Lateral Body Awareness*, which appears next.

INSTRUCTIONS

Since the client will be doing focused movement with their toes and feet, it's ideal to have them be barefoot, not even in socks. Guide them through the following script:

1. *Begin by naming the feeling you would like to work on. You will be working with one foot at a time, alternating the movement of the feet, going back and forth. Hold the tension or the feeling you are working with in your awareness as you listen to my guidance through this exploration.*

2. *Focus on both feet on the ground. Sense the ground underneath your feet. What is one word that describes your awareness in the feet right now?*

3. *Now focus on your right foot. Sense the whole foot. Move it around a bit to feel the contact with the ground.*

4. *Now stretch your fascia underneath your foot by extending the toes upward. Spread your toes and spread the fascia underneath the sole of the foot. Notice the stretch underneath the whole foot. Say out loud this sensation you are feeling right now.*

5. *Now curl the toes under, as if you wanted to pick up a pencil from the ground. Lift the curled toes up just a bit.*

6. *Now stretch out the toes as if you are spreading them along the floor.*

7. *Repeat this motion again. This time feel the texture of the floor as you drag your toes across the floor, curling around the imaginary pencil. [You can actually try this with a pencil or pen; it's a fun and playful variation.]*

8. *In this third round, let's coordinate the movements with your breath. You are still focusing on the same foot. As you exhale, spread and lift the toes of your foot. As you inhale, drag the toes along the floor and curl them in.*

9. *Repeat a fourth time, still coordinating your movements with your breath.*

10. *Now rest and notice your feet. Name out loud what you are sensing. Notice the* [name the feeling the client is working with—e.g., tightness]. *Has that changed?*

11. *Now we will repeat this sequence on the left side, following the same steps. Let's do this very slowly and mindfully.* [Repeat steps 3–9 with the left foot.]

12. *Close your eyes and notice your body. Let's reflect:*

    - *What has changed?*

    - *How do you notice the settling in your body?*

    - *What happened to your* [e.g., tightness, feeling, memory] *at this time?*

    - *Describe in a couple of words your body state.*

One Cycle at a Time—Cross-Lateral Body Awareness

PURPOSE

This is an extension of the previous exercise (*One Cycle at a Time—Moving Feet*). The purpose is to settle the nervous system and to find spaciousness in the somatic experience, so the client can process the associated trauma memory or body sensations.

INSTRUCTIONS

Since the client will be doing focused movement with their toes and feet, it's ideal to have them be barefoot, not even in socks. Guide them through the following script:

1. *Take a moment to hold the tension, body memory, or associated feeling you are working with. Keep this in your awareness as we continue.*

2. *Start with your right foot resting on the floor and your left hand resting on your right thigh. Establish a mental connection with your right foot and left hand.*

3. *Slowly and mindfully stretch your right foot and left hand at the same time, as if you wanted to reach along the floor and your thigh. Feel the stretching of the skin, but more importantly, feel the fascia stretch. Notice any pleasurable sensations that come along with it.*

4. *Now curl the toes of your right foot and curl your left hand into a loose fist at the same time. As you drag your toes across the floor, also feel your fingers as they drag across your thigh and loosely tuck into the fist.*

5. *Take a breath. Now repeat this sequence three times. You want to get into a rhythm with this movement where you feel both the hand and the foot, curling the fingers and toes, at the same time. Go as slowly as you need to.*

6. *Now let's switch to the other side: Place your right hand on your left thigh. Slowly stretch your right hand and your left foot . . . then curl the fingers and toes. Take a breath. Repeat this three times.*

7. *Rest a moment in open attention and receive your body.*

8. *Notice your experience:*

   - *What has changed?*

   - *What are you noticing now?*

   - *Has your* [feeling, tightness, memory, etc.] *shifted? In what ways?*

Safe, Mindful Shaking

PURPOSE

Shaking and tremors are part of our natural nervous system discharge when we are metabolizing stressors in the body. We can include these nervous system movements when we are moving the body toward safety and connection. Some tremors and shakes arise after the trauma response is processed and released. Some shaking we can initiate gently to invite the body's natural processing. The goal is to facilitate a sequenced and safe release and open the information flow within the body.

TIPS

Please note that this type of shaking is designed to be part of being in movement. The moving body will help to process and metabolize the tremors and shakes that are coming up. In this practice we do not want to amplify the shaking too much, as it needs to be connected in a mindful way with the actual movement of the body. Please use caution so as not to overuse this nervous system response.

You might want to mirror the movement with the client to alleviate self-consciousness. This exercise can also be supported by rhythmic, simple beats of music if that is helpful to the client. Encourage a rhythmic shaking and then pause so the client can notice where involuntary movements are occurring within. At that point simply reassure and encourage the client to be with the movements of shaking that are happening. This can facilitate an emotional response.

INSTRUCTIONS

Encourage your client to alternate the shaking movement with frequent pauses to notice and become more aware of their body. Have them study where the body releases and restores. Encourage them to breathe and allow spontaneous movements and sound to happen. Say:

1. *Let's begin by standing comfortably and noticing your body as it is right now. Notice any tension or held or anxious places in the body that you want to work with.*

2. *Start by bouncing your legs in a rhythmic way. Begin a rhythm that you will sustain for a few minutes. Your goal is to start bouncing and then notice where the body wants to shake. This is often an impulse that arises; it can be anywhere in the body.*

3. *Exhale — do not hold your breath. Allow for sound and breath as much as it's comfortable. You want to be in sync with your movements, not exaggerate.*

4. [After two minutes] *Let's pause. Still your body and simply sense where your body is releasing naturally.*

5. *Now start again, this time tuning into your warmed-up body to where the body wants to shake and release. Let that movement be natural, not forced. You are allowing the body to shake, not making it happen.*

6. [After three minutes] *Let's pause again. Notice the breath and body. Where are the subtle tremors occurring? Allow them. If you don't feel any subtle movements, do another cycle of shaking. Follow your body as it wants to shake. If sounds and breath quicken, let that happen.*

7. *Now let's pause again and harvest what is occurring in your body. Again, scan for the subtle levels in the body as it shakes.*

8. Have your client continue this for no more than five cycles, then pause and let the body cool down. Your client might notice very intrinsic movements; invite them to simply feel and sense them.

REFLECTION

Invite the client to respond to the following questions, either by discussing them aloud or by writing in their journal:

- What does the shaking release for you?
- Where and how do you sense the shaking in your body?
- What does this experience help you facilitate?

Releasing One Freeze Cycle at a Time

PURPOSE

When your client is getting activated into a freeze response, their hands and feet may get cold, their body may become stiff, and they might describe a sensation of not being able to move much throughout their whole body. In this case, validate the client's vigilance or fear around being cold, numb, unable to feel the body much, or any associated sensations. The following gentle exercise will help the client to unfreeze the fear response in their body. Introduce it to help the client come back to body sensations and gently regain body awareness. As you introduce this exercise, make sure that you track what is happening in their body while at the same time gently guiding them toward feeling and sensing that body with control.

TIPS

It is important that you start slowly and deliberately, and that you work with micro-movements. Try to avoid fast movements or hurrying up the process. Use language such as *It's okay to go really slow, Take your time really feeling and sensing how the fingers want to move,* or *See if you can do one small little motion with your fingers and see what happens.*

INSTRUCTIONS

Use this script to guide your client:

1. *Start by directing your awareness toward your fingers and hands. Imagine your fingers being surrounded by warm water or warm air.*

2. *Let your fingers move in that warm water, slowly, letting them wake up gently.*

3. *Notice how your breath begins to synchronize with the slow finger movements. Pay attention to the breath deepening and slowing down.*

4. *What is curious to you right now as you move your fingers?*

5. *Where else does the movement want to go? Your hands? Wrists?*

6. *See if you can follow one movement at a time, just enough so you can be with it.*

7. *Let the ease or slow breath be your guide. Just follow what feels right at this moment.*

8. *When there is a natural stopping point, rest and notice.*

9. *What has changed? Do you feel less frozen? What tells you that?*

10. *You can repeat this small motion now with your toes or another part of the body that feels frozen. Only go at the pace of the slowest impulse you can feel in control of. Let go of any ideas of what it "should" be and let the small un-freezing motions guide you.*

11. *What does this process teach you right now?*

Moving, Orienting, and Holding Center Space

PURPOSE

This exercise will help you to regulate by moving your *orienting* impulse. Orienting is an innate, involuntary shift of attention to scan for safety and connection. It is triggered when we feel under threat (Friedman et al., 2009). But it can also be used mindfully to help regulate the threat response. This exercise will help you become conscious of the orienting response and study how movement can deactivate the threat response and help you return to your center.

INSTRUCTIONS

1. Stand with your knees slightly bent, softening your stance.

2. Lift both your arms into a round shape in front of you, having the fingertips lightly touch as if you are hugging a tree. Keep your arms just below shoulder height. See if you can relax your arms and standing position.

3. Breathe in and then, as you exhale, slowly rotate your arms and twist in the waist toward the right. Keep your arms in the rounded shape. The backs of your feet will slightly lift off the ground as you complete the motion.

4. As you inhale, bring your arms in the rounded shape back to the center. Pause here for a full breath cycle (exhale and inhale).

5. Now, with an exhale, rotate to the left until you have completed the twist.

6. With the next inhale, bring the movement back to the center.

7. Bring your arms down to rest. Invite stillness and notice your body.

8. Again, lift your arms into the rounded shape and smoothly twist to the right as you exhale, coordinating the movement with the length of the breath. Inhale as you return to the center. Allow your eyes to travel along with the movement and take in your environment. Let your gaze be soft. You are orienting in the space as you turn and flow with the movement.

9. Take a full breath cycle in the center. Let your gaze softly rest in front of you.

10. Rotate fluidly to the left as you exhale, coordinating the movement with the length of the breath and letting your eyes move through the space around you. As you inhale, return to the center.

11. Repeat the full twist sequence a few times until you feel that the breath, the movement, and the orienting eye gaze are fully coordinated.

12. Then rest your arms alongside your body, rest your gaze slightly downward, and notice the effect of this practice on your nervous system.

REFLECTION

In the space below or in your journal, respond to the following prompt:

- I orient in time and space as I move, and I am _____.

Halt Hand Boundary

PURPOSE

This exercise is designed to help the client become aware of how the body says no and then to physicalize it more consciously. The *halt hand* is a hardwired body motion. We unconsciously use this signal all the time when we want our boundaries respected. You might notice the client making the halt hand when they talk about wanting to set a boundary, wanting to be respected, or experiencing a boundary violation. It can come as a quick, brief gesture, barely noticeable by the client. It is an example of an unconscious somatic movement response to perceived environment stimuli.

INSTRUCTIONS

We can work with the halt hand movement in two ways: by tracking when it comes up spontaneously and by introducing it as a practice.

- **Spontaneously:** When you notice the halt hand come up, pause and feel the impact of the client doing that motion. Then name it out loud, which offers conscious awareness of the motion. Ask the client to repeat the motion and to study what it does, becoming more aware of its purpose.

- **As a practice:** You can invite the client to put one hand up in a gesture of halt or stop. Have them notice what happens as they do. You can model the motion to them or mirror it with them; often that feels safer for the client. This can be done while sitting, standing, or walking.

As the client is exploring this motion, ask:

- *As you hold this hand out, what do you notice?*

- *Where is the hand connected to?*

- *What is the hand saying?*

- *What does this halt hand want to do next?*

Write down what the client's motion communicates.

Boundary Movement

PURPOSE

This exercise helps the client explore what boundaries feel good and right for them. You'll invite the client to experiment with how they have been challenged to set boundaries and to recognize when their boundaries have been crossed.

INSTRUCTIONS

Start by telling your client that they are free to go at their own pace. They will learn how to reestablish boundaries and affirm them through movement explorations. Inform them that if words such as "violated" are too strong, they can simply say "crossed." It's important that the client not be triggered in the trauma story; you want them to be able to explore freely what it feels like to have a boundary crossed and take back that moment of the crossing. Guide your client through the following script.

Noticing the Boundary

1. *You can do this sitting or standing. See what feels right for you.*

2. *Imagine the person who has crossed your boundary. Stay out of the story of what happened and more with the feeling of the boundary being crossed. It can feel energetic and subtle.*

3. *If you feel a tendency to go into the story, simply notice that impulse and mark it for a later time in our therapy work together. Stay with the sensation in your body of the boundary being crossed. Complete this thought: "When I feel my boundary being crossed, I notice my body responding by . . ."*

4. *Notice what happens with your body. Does it feel restricted or smaller? Are there feelings that go with your boundary being crossed? Simply notice at this point. You can take a moment to write down any feelings that get in the way of your being able to sense your body movements. Finish this sentence: "I feel . . ."*

Boundary Exploration

5. *Now let's explore the boundary through movement. Find where in space this boundary could be. You can lift your gaze and survey the space around you. You can lift and move your arms in front of you or around your body and begin to sense where that body boundary is. What are your legs wanting to do? How about your breath—are there any details you notice about your breathing? How is your voice responding? What does your moving body want to do next? Finish these sentences:*

   - *"My gaze tells me . . ."*
   - *"My arms show me . . ."*

- *"My legs want to . . ."*

- *"My breath is . . ."*

- *"My voice needs to . . ."*

- *"My movements are seeking to . . ."*

6. *Go ahead and follow your moving body. Follow your movements and see how the quality of the movement is changing as you physically describe the boundary. Play with qualities of movement such as sharp, soft, edgy, firm, wobbly, and so on. Find different expressions of how you are setting your boundaries and stay tuned into how your feelings change. Fill in the blanks: "When I do _____ [the movement or quality of boundary], I feel _____ [sensation] in my body."*

7. *Explore . . . then find a natural "setting point" from which you feel you can state your boundary. Find that final movement posture and stay with it long enough to see if it feels just right inside. Can you feel a shift?*

8. *Now remember the initial boundary-crossing incident. See if you can state your boundary from this newly found place of empowerment.*

REFLECTION

Invite your client to discuss or journal about this experience and any change they felt.

The Sweep—Unwinding the Freeze

PURPOSE

Working with trauma clients is rewarding but can be somatically challenging. We are resonating beings; we feel and sense with our clients. To recalibrate your own nervous system after a session or a series of sessions, you can do this short practice. Empathy and compassion in the session is a powerful healing tool, but taking a resonant freeze response home is not helpful for you. Make sure to let go of any freeze response you took on during session. You can do this if you have a couple of minutes between clients or take your time after your last client of the day. Repeat this practice anytime you feel a shift into freeze resonance.

INSTRUCTIONS

1. Start standing. Do a quick body scan, from the crown of the head to your feet, or from your feet to your crown. Scan pretty quickly, as if you are sweeping a broom up and down your body. Sense and note places that feel numb, frozen, weird, closed, agitated, or any other sensation.

2. The second time you scan, add a sound, an audible *ahh* or *phew* . . . let the exhale empty completely.

3. The third time you scan, add arm movement. Lift your arms and then drop them with the exhale rapidly. You want a bit of momentum so your attention, sound, breath, and movement all line up.

4. Add some fun into this if it feels right. You can lift your arms over your head and then drop them playfully as if you are a rag doll. As you drop your arms, you might feel your legs wanting to shake along with it. Follow any movement that lets go of the freeze you might have resonated with in your client.

5. Then sit quietly, tracking your body. And then kindly say, "Your freeze is not mine; I am restoring my body flow and ease."

CHAPTER 10

MOVEMENT IN RELATION

"Resonance reveals the deep reality that we are a part of a larger whole [...] that we are created by the ongoing dance within, between, and among us."
—Daniel Siegel, *The Mindful Therapist*

We are relational beings. We live in relation to ourselves, others, and the environment always. The exercises in this chapter explore the theme "standing in relation with," whether a partner, a child, a friend, a coworker, or even nature. They also explore the therapeutic relationship. These tools give insight into how we are in these relationships and what we need to process.

From polyvagal theory we have learned that our social engagement system of connection, belonging, and safety is critical to restore health and well-being. We need to feel in connection to feel our sense of belonging and safety. This embodied safety can be compromised when we are worried in a human relationship or traumatized by events involving nature. Many movement explorations become relational. Early attachment themes are deeply held in how we move our bodies. Exploring these core motions can be a powerful tool to discover the nonverbal expressions of an infant state.

The process of co-regulation in therapy is an essential healing component to developmental and relational trauma. The ability to adjust to the client's needs, shifting moods, expressions, and body motions is critical in conveying safety and receptivity by the therapist. This relational dance has deep roots. Parents and children engage in daily, moment-to-moment exchanges that are nonverbal; as children, we observe, mimic, and respond to our parents' movements. We learn the template of relationship in these unspoken dances with our primary caregivers. We learn somatically that we are received, loved, and welcomed, or not, through the language of gestures and movement in the body. We respond with our moving body to rejection, hurt, and being unloved with tensions, constrictions, and patterns. When, as therapists, we engage the moving repertoire in the therapeutic process, we are evoking these unconscious patterns and language. Therefore, using kindness and mindfulness when working with movement is essential.

Trauma states train us to recognize movements that are threatening at a distance so that we can respond quickly. We learn from our primary caregivers what safe movements look and feel like, and we also learn what dangerous nonverbal expressions feel like so that we can quickly and swiftly defend, run, freeze, or adjust to the danger ahead. Unprocessed trauma states become encoded in our moving body.

No body part is without another. When we carry tensions, memories, bracing patterns, or anxiety in the body, it is never isolated. There is always a tightness in relation to another area. This interrelated body part can shed light on how trauma imprints move through the body and help us to unwind and discover new somatic opening and movement possibilities. The exercise *Explore the Interconnection of Body Parts* is helpful here.

When we begin to move deliberately, we evoke the imprints and responses of the past—along with the new possibility of releasing, processing, and moving beyond that which kept us stuck. Remember to be gentle and slow when you offer these exercises to clients, as they can bring forth potent memories and trauma associations. As always, use your clinical judgment to slow down, resource your client, and pause to process.

Working with the client to know their baseline of being fully connected and safe is an important practice to do *before* exploring the more thematic issues of relationships. It gives a sense of beginning, middle, and end and allows for a more systematic way of tracking the client's progress. They are collecting evidence of their own change process.

Primordial Movement Patterns

"Ehara taku toa i te toa takitahi, engari he toa takitini.
(My strength is not as an individual, but as a collective.)"

—Māori wisdom

Our experience with gravity creates a fundamental trust in experiencing support from others. The *motor reflex* is the bodily response to weight being adjusted and support lost. A newborn is equipped with this primitive reflex in response to loss of support and the experience of falling. When the body senses a shift backward and the weight of the head and is not supported, the *grasping* motor response is elicited. The infant's arms extend and their fingers grasp in order to find a stabilizing entity. When the infant finds support, they learn that they can feel stable again. This primordial pattern of seeking stabilization is also a direct communication with the caregiver and the world. Reaching for another human to receive physiological and emotional support is a basic template of how connections are internalized as safe and nurturing.

When the attachment relationship is injured, these reaching motions are often accompanied by sadness, grief, or anger. Reflexes can be retained as body memories and get expressed later in the nervous system as incomplete responses and emotional patterns. If the reflex is retained it can be felt as oversensitivity to sound, touch, and smells, even an inability to overcome inner hypervigilance. However, what was not given in infancy can be reimagined through movement. These primordial movement patterns can be worked with in the safe therapeutic container. The *Reaching and Relating* exercise in this chapter does just that.

Movement and Nature

"All living processes owe their lineage to the movement of water. Our implicit preexistent memory beginning with the first cell, lies in the mysterious deep, quietly undulating, circulating, nourishing this aquatic being on its mission to planet Earth. God is not elsewhere, but is moving through our cells and in every part of us with its undulating message."

—Emilie Conrad, "Continuum Movement"

Another important exploration in movement is our relationship to the natural world. Being in nature or imagining being in nature can be a very powerful resource when healing from trauma. Yet, climate change and the shift in habitats has many clients grieving over and feeling helpless and anxious about the natural world. Exercises such as *Eco-Movement* and *Take Your Senses Walking* are helpful to explore the trauma experienced by the client and restore a sense of trust.

We relate through our proprioception to the space around us. We sense how far or close and how connected we are when in nature. We often describe being in nature as calming, invigorating, connecting; we are in awe of the beauty of a sunset, the magnificence of a mountain vista, the refreshing rhythm of the surf, or the still whispers of a forest. For many trauma clients, nature is a safe place, a sanctuary, away from humans and possible hurt or remembering the traumatic past.

On one of my own wilderness hikes I was fortunate to be guided by a former veteran. Deeply knowledgeable about the Australian outback, he was calmly guiding me and my family with two young teens through rough cliffs, narrow river tunnels, and steep ravines. We had to jump into dark, deep water from harrowing heights. My fear level rose with each of the challenges. But our guide was calm, trusting the land and his body as he led us onward. His assuring hand was steady and his body relaxed more with each hour that we tracked deeper into the wilderness. He felt at home in this rugged terrain.

After a customary tea break, enjoying the stunning vista of the Blue Mountains, I asked him what connected him to the land and being a guide. He said that he sought it for healing. After his multiple deployments into war zones, he needed a safe place to heal. Nature was his guide. We talked about his war experiences and the pain in his eyes was palpable—a look I have seen many times over in my trauma clients. It was in relation to nature's rhythms, sounds, and stillness that he could feel himself again.

Nature is the ultimate movement partner. We can observe how the wind rustles in the trees, swaying the branches in rhythms of soft arches. We can witness heavy rain carving small temporary rivers in a muddy footpath, pooling small water puddles, inviting a childlike desire to stomp into it. We slow and breathe as we take in the scenery, the mind unfurling with each step we climb up a hill or lazily meander through a forest. Our connection with nature, the way we move our body through the landscape, reminds us again that we are connected.

Many of the practices in this book can be offered outside for the client to practice in relation to nature. This simple shift of relating with the natural world opens our perception and lets us discover the connections of inner rhythms forgotten or masked by trauma symptoms and emotional pain. Many therapists include ecotherapy in their trauma approaches, and these might be some additional tools you can bring with you. See *Eco-Movement* and *Take Your Senses Walking* in this chapter for direct movement in nature.

Working with Space

"Silence is the soul's break for freedom."

—David Whyte, *Crossing the Unknown Sea*

How we move through space is about how we move our body and belongings through the world. Working with space and the quality of spaciousness can generate a profound resource and antidote to feelings such as overwhelm, fear, and anger. When our feeling body becomes too much, working with the physical space around us as awareness practice is helpful. Intense emotions can make us feel collapsed inside and we stop perceiving that we are in relationship with the larger world around us. However, we can learn to rest and trust the space around us by moving with the physical space as we perceive it, noticing where we are and how we feel within that physical space. We are used to moving in space every day, but we don't usually shift into the awareness of space. Your client can practice this in the exercise *Extending into Spaciousness* in this chapter. Learning to reframe one's experience from a new vantage point is the first part of working with space.

The second part of working with space is discovering the spaciousness inside of us that is not occupied by fear, overwhelm, frozenness, and other feelings associated with trauma. Trauma experiences can make us feel small, collapsed, tight, or withdrawn. In these somatic states we can feel limited in our emotional and physical experience. When working with trauma clients, you want to help them find the impulse of wanting to feel themselves extending back out after they have felt withdrawn. *Extending into Spaciousness* is a good practice for this.

This quality of spaciousness as a body-mind state can become a powerful healing experience. When we move our body in consciousness of space outside and space within, we are accessing a deeper calm that is not just about self-regulation. This deeper spaciousness affirms that we are here and in a deep relationship with our outer and inner nature. We are meant to move, explore, and discover.

Moving Smooth or Rough

PURPOSE

This relational tool will help your client discover how they have been impacted relationally by their trauma experience. They will explore a quality within that they notice due to their trauma history—for example, feeling unsafe, anxious, and awkward around others. Relationships have many textures, but smooth and rough are two qualities of being that we can translate into movement and learn about.

INSTRUCTIONS

Explain to your client that they will explore the movement qualities of smooth and rough, which can also describe the textures of our relationships. If they don't like the word "rough," invite them to substitute "uneven," "jagged," "shy," or another word that they want to explore in contrast. Guide them through the following script.

Qualities of Moving

1. *First, let's get to know the movement qualities of smoothness and roughness.*

2. *Either standing or sitting, use your hands, your arms, or your whole body to explore the rough qualities of movement. What are they?*

3. *Fill in the blank: "When I move roughly, I feel _____."*

4. *Next, explore the movement quality of smoothness. Find a motion that moves smoothly. Notice the change of pace and texture that comes with it.*

5. *Fill in the blank: "When I move smoothly, I feel _____."*

Exploring the Edges of the Relationship

6. *Now shift to working with a relationship in your life right now. Bring to mind that person. Notice a relational pattern of rough edges, such as being awkward or not yourself around that person. You might be feeling that you are holding back. In other words, you do not feel a smooth connection with that person.*

7. *Notice what happens in your body when you bring this person to your conscious mind. What happens with your movement qualities? Are they wanting to get larger, smaller, cold, or fiery?*

8. *Fill in the blanks:*

  - *"I have a _____ [relationship quality] relationship with this person."*

  - *"I notice that when I am with this person, I feel _____."*

  - *"I can't fully express _____ and I notice I am _____ in their presence."*

9. *Now, find a movement that has a rough quality to it. You can move your hands, arms, or whole body. See if that matches the relational quality you feel in this person's presence.*

10. *Move for a few minutes until you notice a shift, then pause and notice. Describe how you are feeling now.*

Exploring the Potential of the Relationship

11. *Now imagine yourself how you would like to be with that person. Allow your movements to reflect smooth qualities. Play with different variations of how to move smoothly.*

12. *When you are ready, fill in the blanks:*

  - *"I notice that when I move smoothly, I feel _____."*

  - *"I would like to bring forth this _____ [quality] in myself in this relationship."*

REFLECTION

Discuss or have the client write in their journal about this experience.

Boundary Practice

PURPOSE

This tool is designed to help you study the boundaries that have been crossed on a somatic and movement level. It will help elicit the direct experience so that the client can find what needs to happen to reestablish the boundaries necessary to feel safe and protected.

INSTRUCTIONS

1. Have the client take a body posture that feels like a baseline position. Then invite the client to think of a moment when their boundaries were violated or not respected. Notice their body response.

2. Ask the following questions very slowly. Leave time in between each question for the client to respond in motion. Ask each question twice: The first time you ask, notice the client's initial response. The second time, truly study the body's response.

   - *Can you find your skin boundary? You can use palpate motions on your body to help you ground and be in direct contact with your skin boundary.*

   - *Can you find the movement that describes the body boundary?*

   - *Can you find the movement that describes your energetic boundary needs?*

   - *Can you find/hold/defend/commit to the boundary that you need from now on?*

   - *What stands in the way for you to assert the boundary that you need?*

3. Notice any frozen or held places in the client's body. When you notice one, either talk about it or ask the client to find a movement to express it.

4. When the client is finished moving, ask them: *If this posture and movement could speak, what would it say now?*

Pushing Hands

PURPOSE

This a powerful relational movement whereby your client can discover their own boundaries in relation to another person. Pushing and moving together is about both boundaries and relationships. Your client will negotiate through playful movement what it means to be in a safe and boundaried relationship. The goal is to study the right and safe contact that is met with respect. This is *not* a reenactment of a boundary being violated. This is about establishing what feels right, safe, and connected in a relationship with another person.

TIPS

If skin-to-skin contact feels too evocative for you or the client, you can place a thin pillow between the hand contact. Help the client realize that boundaries have been violated as part of the trauma experience. Pause and let the client resource their body. In these moments, it can be helpful to simply stay present, drop the hand contact, and affirm that the client has the control over this exercise.

INSTRUCTIONS

1. Stand (or sit) across from each other.

2. Invite the client into this mindful, playful exercise that involves pushing and moving together. Instruct the client to go slow and notice the cues of their body. Affirm that you both can take a pause at any time and will be pausing frequently to notice and study the movement impact. Let the client sense and feel into their experience. Laughter and play can often come with this exercise, as well as shame, awkwardness, and shyness. Set up ground rules of safety and respect.

3. To begin, lift your hands up as an invitation for the client to meet your hands with theirs. Check whether direct hand-to-hand contact feels unsafe or uncomfortable. If so, adjust. You can use a pillow between your hands so there is no skin-to-skin contact.

4. When the client meets your hands, invite them to notice the contact.

5. Then instruct them to gently push toward your hands, to feel their weight leaning forward and meeting the contact. At the same time, you will meet that contact as if you are a mirror. Your job is to respond to the pushing by delivering just the right amount of resistance so the client can feel the contact, not more or less.

6. Invite your client to move their weight back and forth so that there is a gentle forward-and-backward motion. At times the contact will feel looser and at other times firmer. Stay with the movement they are initiating. Study the impact.

7. As they are moving and exploring, ask:

   - *What is the right amount of contact for you to feel safe and boundaried?*
   - *What tells you inside your body that this is safe?*
   - *Where is the optimum point of contact and the right amount of movement?*
   - *What is the quality of connection right now?*

8. Then find a resting place. You can both mindfully drop your hands by your sides.

9. Take a step back into your own physical kinesphere. Have your client take a breath and sense into their body.

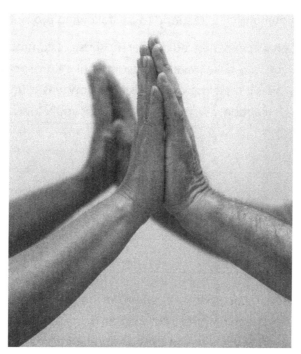

REFLECTION

After this exploration, have your client answer the following questions in their journal:

- What are your body boundaries now that you have been engaging in the pushing hands?
- What tells you that you are safe inside your body?
- What do you notice for yourself?
- What do you notice in the relationship? More connection or less?

Kinesphere Moving Boundaries

PURPOSE

The objective of this exercise is to notice and explore your *kinesphere*, the personally felt space around your body. Think of it as an invisible space of comfort and safety that you need to feel good. The kinesphere varies for each person. There are family, cultural, and societal norms that have an impact on how we perceive our personal and collective kinesphere.

INSTRUCTIONS

Use the space provided or your journal to respond to the following prompts:

1. Remember a time when you experienced a different sense of communal space than you were used to (for example, you may have traveled to a different culture or moved into a living space with new roommates). Was it too close or too distant? How was your own perception of space different from others' perceptions? What was that like for you? How did that impact your sense of connection and safety?

   _____

   _____

   _____

   _____

2. We negotiate our personal space every day when we are with others. Think of standing in a long line. What happens when people want to cut the line or are anxious and move closer to your body? In trauma experiences we have our safety boundaries breached, and the sense of your personal kinesphere might change or feel nonexistent. Draw or write about your kinesphere and its boundaries.

Moving Boundary Sequence

PURPOSE

Interpersonal trauma experiences can include physical or energetic boundary violations. Learning to recognize what these boundary crossings have been and how to reestablish the boundaries is a process. Clients often don't know how to feel their boundaries at first and need time and space to sense them in relation to others. In this exercise, your client will take time to sense what a boundary means to them.

INSTRUCTIONS

This exercise is divided into four steps. In the first two steps, the client will explore the boundary they want to create for themselves without relating to you. It's helpful if they first feel into what their boundary actually is. Allow them to experiment with movements that establish a boundary. Let them know that physical boundaries are not static but move with each person and depending on the situation. Remind them that by knowing their boundary they can work on restoring their personal space.

For some clients those first two steps might be enough; it is important to check at that point if the client wants to affirm the boundary in the relationship. If they want to take the next two steps, notice any shifts and feelings that might arise. You can add to step 3 an answer if the client is open to it, such as *I will respect your boundary*. Keep in mind that affirming a body boundary can be initially triggering.

Step 1: Noticing How the Boundary Feels

1. *Stand and move in the room freely as you wish.*

2. *Feel your body in relation to the space that you are in. Notice:*

   - *Does your body have a boundary?*

   - *How are you feeling about your boundary right now?*

   - *Is the boundary felt close to your skin or farther away from your skin?*

   - *How far does your boundary extend?*

3. *Now, fill in the blank with a descriptive word or phrase: "My boundary is _____."*

Step 2: Moving the Boundary

4. *Start moving your arms as if you are drawing your personal kinesphere around your body. You can move all around your body—below, above, and sideways.*

5. *How far does it extend?*

6. *Now, fill in the blanks with a descriptive word or phrase:*

   • *"My moving boundary makes me feel _____."*

   • *"When I move _____ [quality of movement] to affirm my boundary, I am saying _____ [statement about what this boundary is standing for]."*

Step 3: Moving the Boundary in Relation to the Therapist

7. *Now let's stand opposite each other and affirm the boundary you just discovered. Draw with your arms and whole body what your personal kinesphere is at this moment. Feel what it is like to affirm your needs right now. Let your body affirm your new boundary.*

8. *Now, fill in the blanks:*

   • *"I need you to respect this boundary: _____ [descriptive word or phrase]."*

   • *"This is what I need: _____ [state your need as you describe a movement that goes along with it]."*

9. *[You, the therapist, can reply:] I will respect/am respecting your boundary.*

10. *[After a few moments, you can prompt:] Take a moment and stand still . . . absorb what just happened. Feel into this new experience.*

11. *How is your body right now? Do you notice any shifts or feelings that come with this right now? Fill in the blank: "I notice _____."*

Step 4: Moving the Boundary in Relation to the Other Person (Imagined)

12. *Now imagine your new boundary in relation to the person who has crossed it. Feel into the newly established boundary. Move your body to establish the new boundary again. Feel the strength and the clarity in the movements that feel right to you in establishing this boundary.*

13. *Imagine saying to this person: "This is my boundary:_____ [descriptive word or phrase] and you have no right to cross it."*

14. *See what other movements come along with this statement and feeling that you are affirming. You can repeat the statement or add your own words now.*

15. *What wants to be said as you feel this new boundary in relation to the other person? What is your truth here right now?*

REFLECTION

Have the client use their journal or the worksheet that follows to make a drawing of their body boundary and write down any words or insights that have come up.

Body Boundary Drawing

Use the space below to draw your body boundary and add any words or insights that have come up. This can be done as you reflect on the *Moving Boundary Sequence* exercise.

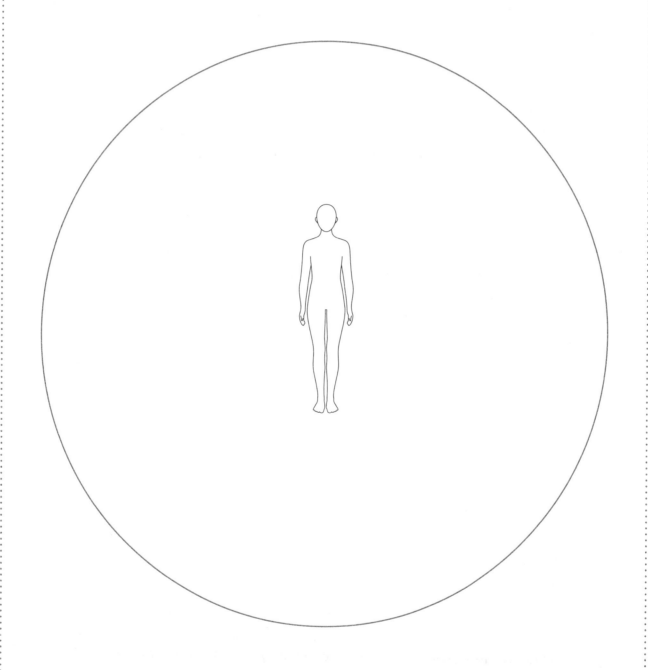

Exploring the Right Distance

PURPOSE

This is a dyadic exercise. When one person moves, it impacts the need for a different boundary for the other person. The purpose is to explore how the needs of closeness and distance can shift, how closeness and distance are negotiated, and how the perceptions shift.

TIPS

Your role is to move in response to the client and in reflection. This allows the client to learn what happens to their own sense of physical space and safety when you move. Can they reestablish it when they move? You might set a timer, if you are more comfortable having a definite stop. Or you can find a natural stopping point.

INSTRUCTIONS

The goal is for the client to notice their own kinesphere in motion and in relation to others, and to reassert their own sense of safety. Be respectful of each other's movements and explorations. This exercise requires mindful awareness. Your client needs to learn about what feels right for them and how to respect the other person's personal kinesphere. Make small adjustments and allow for some playfulness.

1. Ensure your client has a writing utensil and either their journal or a copy of the worksheet that is included at the end of this exercise.

2. Begin by telling your client, *Feel your standing body and how you are right now. Tune into your personal physical space and notice your body.*

3. Ask the client to make a drawing in the first box of the worksheet: *How do you experience your personal space right now? What would that look like? Draw and name your experience.*

4. Next, stand across from each other. Begin to move mindfully. No words, just movement. Allow for nonverbal communication. You can ask, *What is the right distance for you right now?*

5. Notice the client adjusting, such as moving farther away or a bit closer. Then move in relation to the client's new position. This can be a movement toward or away.

6. The client will notice this adjustment and respond. They may move away or closer.

7. This time, stay in the position you are in and wait. Notice whether the client makes another adjustment. Ask them, *What do you notice? What feelings come with this position? What happens with your body boundary?*

8. Next, move closer to or farther from the client (whatever feels right to you) but ask the client to stay put. Then ask the client, *What happens with your sense of distance? Where is your boundary now?*

9. Both of you should make one final adjustment to what feels just right. Invite the client to study what happens inside.

10. Ask the client to make a drawing in the second box on the worksheet: *What is the most affirming and right distance for you?* They might include themselves, you, or another person in this drawing.

Exploring the Right Distance

You can use the space here or your own journal to draw and write your reflections during the exercise *Exploring the Right Distance.*

1. How do you experience your personal space right now? What would that look like? Draw and name your experience in the box below.

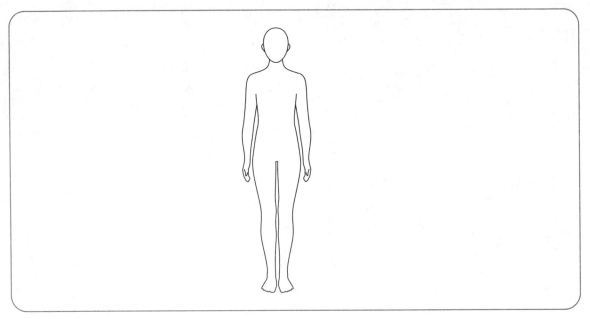

2. What is the most affirming and right distance for you? Draw it in the next box. You might include yourself, your therapist, or another person in your drawing.

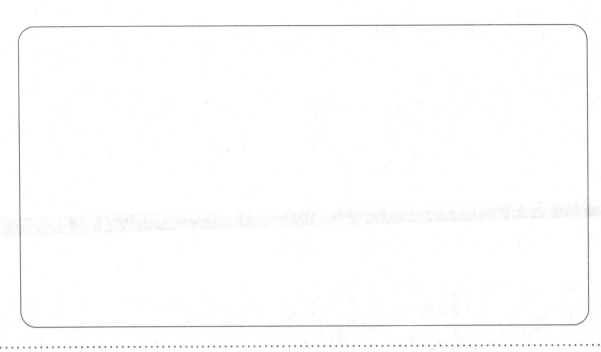

Mirroring

PURPOSE

Mirroring is a classic dance movement therapy technique. It enables us to sense and feel into the world of the other, especially when words are not available. We can sense through our own moving body what it might be like to live in their skin. This can get us close to feeling empathy, which is often described as "walking in another person's shoes."

INSTRUCTIONS

Your focus in this practice is to mirror the client as accurately as possible so they can see themselves in your movements. Allow for playful movements and different rhythms, such as fast and slow. Notice subtle changes. This exercise is done standing and facing each other. Say:

1. *Imagine you are standing in front of a mirror. It's the early morning and you are getting ready for the day. It is a private moment and you are taking care of your body and being with yourself. You will be brushing your hair, washing your face, and brushing your teeth. Allow yourself to be playful.*

2. *Slowly lift your right arm and pretend that you are holding a brush, combing your hair very slowly. Go super slow, as if every moment is in slow motion.*

3. [Track these movements and see if you can mimic the client's exact movements, as if you are the mirror feeding back what you are receiving.]

4. *Bring your brushing to a close . . . check the mirror.*

5. *Now continue getting ready for the day, completing any other tasks that you want to explore. This might be washing your face, smiling at yourself—whatever actions you want to do.*

6. [Again, mirror as closely as possible. If the client's movements become too fast or too complicated, you can ask them to slow down and come back to a very simple task.]

7. *Close your eyes and notice what it was like to see yourself through the eyes of the other.*

REFLECTION

Afterward, discuss what that experience was like and what your client discovered.

Reaching and Relating

PURPOSE

In this exercise, your client will explore the innate capacity, need, and motivation to reach toward and receive support, and then study where this has been denied or injured. If there are early attachment relationship themes, explore gently so the client can rediscover what needs to happen to restore basic trust and safety in the body. This exercise will help to process these sensitivities of need for connection and fear of rejection through movement. Embodying these needs will lead toward more resilience.

TIPS

Make sure you go very slowly and mindfully. These movements are primal and preverbal and can evoke strong somatic experiences. You want to track the client's moving toward what they need, not bring up traumatic memories. Have the client play with these motions to discover and feel in their body what wants to be completed. For example, reaching toward a person asks them to feel that reach and also imagine that this reach is being answered. You can support these movements by reaching out verbally and having them mindfully study it. If safe touch is permitted and consented to, you can also physically support the reaching arm. This in itself can feel healing and grounding for the client.

INSTRUCTIONS

Use your sensitivity with this powerful exercise and go slow. The goal is to understand how internalized safety has been injured and how the client can reinstate this sense of reaching in safety by doing these motions consciously. Explore mindfully the different kinds of reaching out and grasping. Study the feelings and sensations that are being evoked. The client can do this sitting or lying down; note that lying down adds an extra vulnerability. Say:

1. *We will be exploring movements of reaching out for support and connection. You may discover relationship patterns that have been imprinted in your body.*

2. *Slow down and become mindful of your body. Breathe slowly . . . open your senses.*

3. *Slowly lift your arms and begin to reach toward, meaning you are stretching out your arms in front of you. You can imagine a person you're reaching toward, if that's helpful.*

4. *Stay with your arms stretched out as you reach and notice how your arms feel. Are they heavy, light, buoyant, or any other sensations that go along with it? Are there any feelings or images that come along with this?*

5. *Slowly return your arms back to a neutral position alongside your body and rest. Close your eyes and notice your experience.*

6. *Repeat the motion of reaching out again, but this time add a grasping motion at the end of the reaching. Allow any movement that wants to arise in your body . . . just let it be.*

7. *Notice your head and neck. What movements or sensations do you notice in that area of the body? What feelings arise?*

8. *Allow your movements to spontaneously guide you. There might be a word or a sound that wants to go with it. Explore different kinds of reaching; what kinds of qualities can you explore here?*

9. *Now let your arms rest and notice again your body's responses.*

REFLECTION

Afterward, invite the client to discuss or write about their experience by filling in the blanks:

- When I reach, I want _____.
- When I see you, I need _____.
- When you reach for me, I feel _____.
- When I reach for you, I feel _____.
- My arms are _____ when I reach.
- My eyes are _____ when I reach.
- My body is _____ when I reach.
- I need you to _____ when I reach.
- I will no longer _____ when I reach.

Eco-Movement

PURPOSE

Allow yourself to be taught by the nature around you. See if you can open your senses to perceiving nature *as* movement. You are working on building an internal repertoire to sense and feel and learning how nature can help you with that process.

INSTRUCTIONS

1. Pick a spot in nature where you can connect with a tree (or another kind of plant). You can sit or stand in front of that tree.

2. Observe the tree. Take in its shapes, textures, and colors.

3. Imagine its age, its history, how it got here.

4. Consider how the tree is connected underground with roots you can't see.

5. Soften your gaze and notice if there is any movement in the branches or leaves. How is the wind making contact with the tree? Let yourself see the movement that is here right now.

6. Notice your breath response. You don't have to "do" anything; simply observe and be with the wind and your own breath. How is your breath changing right now?

7. Now lift one hand and mimic one motion you are observing, as if you are becoming the mirror of that leaf or branch.

8. Close your eyes and let that movement quality permeate. What is that movement inviting you into?

9. Notice how your body wants to continue or pause.

10. Then open your eyes and pick another area on the tree that you see moving. Again, lift your hand to move with the tree. Let this movement be a teacher for *how* to move.

11. Follow the movement and see how it calms, settles, or regulates where you are at.

12. When you feel that you are finished, simply rest. Let your attention be open and soft. Notice the change in your nervous system. What did you discover?

13. Draw a picture of you and the tree moving. You can let it be a childlike picture; this is not about creating a "good" drawing but expressing what you notice and feel. Go ahead and express the moving feelings and the tree in the space below or in your journal.

Take Your Senses Walking

PURPOSE

This is a walking exercise to open all your senses in relation to the environment around you. In this practice, you will walk and sense at the same time: seeing, smelling, hearing, tasting, touching.

INSTRUCTIONS

1. Take all your senses on a mindful walk. Let the walking be slow and deliberate so you can begin to rotate your awareness through your senses. Really feel yourself moving through the environment.

2. As you walk, say inside or out loud:

   - I am sensing with my _____ that I am _____.
   - I am feeling in my _____ that I can _____.
   - I hear _____.
   - I see _____.
   - I smell _____.
   - I taste _____.
   - I touch _____.

3. As you walk with your senses, notice how your body perceptions change. Is there more connection with your environment? Is your body wanting to move quicker or slower? Are there movement impulses that arise? Feel your whole body connect with your senses into the environment. What is different now?

Jaw and Pelvis

PURPOSE

This practice is to help unfreeze the jaw. The jaw holds a lot of our daily tension. We brace in the jaw, holding feelings in or keeping them out. We grind our teeth when we are anxious and anticipating. When we work with a tension in one part of the body we also can explore how it relates to another part. In this exercise you will explore the relationship between the jaw and the pelvis.

INSTRUCTIONS

1. Get into a relaxed body position where you are not holding up your body. You can either lie down or sit. Have your legs stretched out or your feet on the floor with your knees supported.

2. Become aware of your jaw position. Is it tight, loose, numb?

3. Now gently let your jaw open slowly. Feel the slow opening and lengthening that happens as you do so . . . then close the jaw very slowly. Repeat this opening and closing in a smooth way. Explore what happens in your breath as you do so.

4. Next, explore the lateral movement of the jaw. First, allow your jaw to open ever so slightly. Then add a slight side-to-side motion. Let that movement be smooth, not mechanical in any way.

5. Rest and sense for a moment.

6. Next, if you are lying down, place your feet on the ground, knees bent, and let your legs fall toward each other so that your lower back is relaxed. If you are seated, rest your feet on the floor and sit upright. See if you can be relaxed and alert at the same time.

7. Tilt your pelvis very slightly, moving it away from the floor and then toward the navel. Make this a very small and smooth motion.

8. Rest and sense for a moment.

9. Now move your jaw open and closed and side to side with the pelvis motion. Explore the movements as they coordinate with each other. Let the jaw and pelvis move together. See what happens as you do so.

10. Rest and sense for a moment. What are you noticing about your jaw now? What has happened to the freeze?

REFLECTION

In the space below or in your journal, write about what you discovered about the jaw and pelvis relationship.

_____

_____

_____

_____

Explore the Interconnection of Body Parts

PURPOSE

In this exercise, you will explore two areas in your body that are related. It's a way to learn about the patterns your body develops in response to strong feelings or experiences. These gentle explorations will allow you to study your moving body on your own terms.

INSTRUCTIONS

Go slowly and mindfully. Pause when you want more information or to journal your thoughts. Stay connected with your own interest, and rest when you feel it has been enough.

1. Tune into your body and notice the area that's speaking to you right now. It could be a tension or an area that simply wants attention.

2. Find a movement that brings more awareness to that area. Move in small and mindful ways, exploring what you notice as you do so.

3. Ask yourself: What is familiar? Are there feelings that go with it?

4. Now pause and study if there is another area in your body that seems to be connected. Where do you sense it? What are you noticing about this part right now?

5. Now, move that area mindfully. Be open to discovery.

6. Pause again and sense how the two areas are now connecting. If they could have a dialogue, what would they say to each other? Are they supportive of each other? In opposition? Is one a protective area or body part?

7. Now move the two areas together, if possible, and see what you can learn. Pause and notice at times. Observe what comes up.

REFLECTION

Write down your insights and discoveries by filling in the blanks and elaborating:

- I discovered that my body area of _____

  is connected with _____.

- Here is what I learned about this relationship:

  _____

  _____

Facing Safely (Face, Chest, Heart, and Hands)

PURPOSE

When faced with overwhelming feelings, shame, or awkwardness, your client can learn how to come into a safe relationship with "facing" another person with this exercise. From the polyvagal perspective we understand how important facial engagement is to help regulate the emotional inner activation of the nervous system. In this exercise your client will consciously connect the corridor of awareness between the eyes, mouth, whole face, neck, chest, heart, and hands to help release any trauma memory. Because this is such a primal way of connecting with another human, when this somatic pathway is interrupted it can bring forth feelings of shame, emotional retreat, and fear.

TIPS

Help your client by offering not to sit right in front of them initially. Being dyadically opposed can bring somatic activation and can feel confrontational. You want your client to start out with their inner experience, getting used to working with the subtle hand movement. Once they are comfortable you can ask the client if they want to try this exercise facing you. Track for any signs of emotional charge or somatic bracing, such as holding the breath, pulling inward, or tightening their body posture. If you see this, then move again to another position not facing them directly to ease the tension.

INSTRUCTIONS

You will teach your client how to be emotionally regulated when facing another person. The subtle pulsing movements of their hands will help them to metabolize any small stressors they might feel. Take your time, go slow, and study what arises for them. This is about your client learning how to feel safe in connection and that they can work with one stressor at a time through hand movement. Make sure you remind them to connect with the awareness of their face, neck, and chest *as* they do this movement mindfully. Be kind and patient as you guide them through the five parts of this exercise using the following script.

Part 1

1. *We'll begin by sitting down, across from each other. Cast your eyes downward so you can be with the experience.*

2. *Become aware of me and where I am in relation to you. You can ask me to move slightly away, or move aside, if it feels too charged to sit face-to-face. We will wait until you are comfortable to do so.*

Part 2

3. *Have a relaxed, upright posture. But keep your eyes cast down to tune into your inner awareness. Rest your hands in your lap with your palms facing up.*

4. *Become aware of your whole face, the front of the neck, the upper chest, your heart center, and your inner hands. Simply notice what is here in your body. Take a baseline of awareness. What is present in these regions of awareness right now?*

5. *Fill in the blanks out loud as I say them:*

    - *"I notice that my face feels _____."*
    - *"I notice that the front of my neck feels _____."*
    - *"When I swallow, I sense _____."*
    - *"I notice that my upper chest feels _____."*
    - *"When I breathe into my chest, I sense _____."*
    - *"I notice that my heart feels _____."*
    - *"I notice that my inner palms feel _____."*

Part 3

6. *Now think about a situation where facing another being is a challenge for you. It could be facing me right here. Or it might be standing up to a certain person in your life or even facing a situation that is difficult.*

7. *Notice the regions of your body you just worked with. What has changed? Again, fill in the blanks: I notice that my [face, neck, chest, heart, hands] feel[s] _____. It reminds me of _____."*

Part 4

8. *Now begin to slowly and mindfully stretch the palms of your hands as if you wanted to overstretch the back of your hands. Begin to open each finger . . . and spread them apart from each other.*

9. *When you have reached the maximum stretch point, feel into the fascia in your inner palms, and then slowly release and let your hands naturally curl back on their own.*

10. *Begin to add your breath with this movement. As you inhale, begin to stretch your palms. You can do one palm at a time or both at the same time. Pause at the end with your palms extended. Then exhale slowly and let your hands naturally curl in. As you exhale fully, rest for a moment and feel the release in the center of your palms.*

11. *Synchronizing with your breath, stretch and release the inner palms five times.*

12. *Again, fill in the blanks:*

    - *"I notice _____."*

- *"As I remember the challenge in my life, my body now feels _____."*
- *"The part of my body that is the calmest right now is my _____ [face, neck, chest, hands, heart]."*

Part 5

13. *Take a moment now to relax. Open your eyes and look around to orient yourself. Try to see with curiosity, as if you are seeing the room for the first time. What is novel right now?*

14. *Now bring another person into your visual orienting. This might be me, or you can imagine the person in your life that you are having difficulty facing. What do you notice about your own face, neck, and heart region as you now include the other face?"*

15. *[If you notice that your client is still activated, have them repeat part 4 as they face you or the imagined person.]*

16. *Describe what you notice now:*

    - *What has changed?*

    - *What is helpful right now?*

    - *What do you notice in your breathing rhythm?*

The Rhythms of the Relationship

PURPOSE

This exercise can help shift early psychological patterns. Trauma experiences interrupt the sense of wanting to be close, or *move with* someone, just as it might enhance *moving against* or *moving toward*. By making these movement patterns explicit, the client can become more conscious of how these movements may be impacting close relationships—they can embody and re-remember the personal meaning that they have learned to attach to them.

TIPS

It can be helpful to imagine yourself as a projection screen. You are not in the therapist role during this exploration. You are a neutral guide, and you want to allow the client to explore freely. You can explain this to the client, asking them to release you temporarily from the therapist role.

INSTRUCTIONS

This exercise can be done either sitting or standing, but it's more effective if both of you can stand in a neutral position that will serve as your baseline. Guide the client through the sequence with mindful pacing. Pause in silence in between the questions, and allow the client to respond in movement. Encourage them to be present and go slow, studying these patterns before making any meaning. Use the following script.

Introduction

1. *In this exercise, you will be exploring three basic relational patterns: moving toward, moving away, and moving against. In between each of the movements, you will come back to a baseline neutral position, study your experience, and write down what you are feeling.*

2. *You can use me or an object to stand in for the person in the relationship you're wanting to explore. Just remember that this exploration is about your internalized patterns in relation to that other person in your life, not to be confused with the relationship you have with me. Please be respectful and aware of my personal boundaries, just as I will be of yours.*

Part 1: Moving Toward

3. *Slowly approach* [me/the object, whatever represents the relationship]. *As you do so, notice what comes up. Go really slowly so you can truly feel and sense the changes that are happening in your body.*

4. *As I ask these questions, respond in movement:*
   - *Where in your body do you feel a desire to connect?*
   - *How do your feelings change as you get closer?*
   - *What is the right boundary as you move toward* [me/the object]?
   - *How can you tell in your body what is the right distance?*
   - *What comes up for you as a theme or memory as you move toward* [me/the object]?

5. *Come back to the baseline position and journal your responses to the questions.* [If needed, repeat the previous list of questions as they write.]

Part 2: Moving Away

6. *Return to your baseline. From your baseline slowly move away from* [me/the object]. *As I ask these questions, simply respond in movement:*
   - *What is the impact of moving away?*
   - *What does this remind you of?*
   - *Where in your body do you feel a yes?*
   - *Where in your body do you feel a no?*

7. *Come back to baseline and journal your responses to the questions.* [Repeat the previous list of questions if needed.]

Part 3: Moving Against

8. *Now, return to your baseline again. From your baseline, slowly move against* [me/the object]. *Find a movement that symbolizes "against." Be mindful not to touch* [me/the object]; *this is a symbolic movement, such as lifting a hand or an arm. Again, as I ask these questions, simply respond in movement:*
   - *Notice what tension arises in the body.*
   - *From where in your body do you mobilize against?*
   - *What feelings come with this motion?*
   - *What part of your body is the main mobilizer? Hands, arms, feet, legs, face?*
   - *What sound or voice do you hear inside as you do this movement?*

9. *Come back to baseline and journal your responses to the questions.* [Repeat the previous list of questions if needed.]

Part 4: Return to Baseline

10. [After the movement exploration ends, mark that you're switching out of this role as the projection screen and are stepping back into being a therapist.] *Return now to baseline. You can sit or lie down if you need to shake and move your body from these patterns. Study your experience and notice what is present here:*

    • *What was helpful to realize?*

    • *What movements feel easy and accessible?*

    • *What movements were difficult or had a no or taboo associated with them?*

REFLECTION

In writing, have the client answer:

• What did you learn about these patterns?

• What has been helpful in the past?

• What no longer serves?

Extending into Spaciousness

PURPOSE

This healing exercise is designed to help you experience extending yourself into a spacious quality. It may bring up physical, emotional, and possibly spiritual resources that you have not yet discovered. Allow yourself to be curious and open and explore these new possibilities. Movement is both an expression and an agent of the change process itself. Be inquisitive and allow yourself to not get stuck in resistance or dismissing thoughts.

INSTRUCTIONS

Be very mindful as you move with this exercise. Read the instructions all the way through first, so you have an idea of where you're going. Then return to the beginning and read each step slowly, pausing to answer each question silently to yourself. At the end, you will need your journal to reflect in writing.

Part 1: Take a Somatic Baseline

1. Where do you feel constriction or tightness in your body right now? How do you notice yourself in this constriction?

2. Now stand up and connect with your feet and the ground beneath you. What do you notice taking up this physical space?

3. Notice the space around you. Notice the walls, the details in the room. Let yourself look around.

4. Remember that beyond these walls is more room, space, or nature.

5. Fill in the blank: As I feel into the physical room, I sense _____.

6. Now sense back into your body. Where in your body are you feeling the constriction or tightness right now? It might have shifted already.

Part 2: Reaching into Space

7. Bring awareness to your hands and fingers and start reaching them into the space around you. Let your arms follow.

8. Continue very slowly and mindfully reaching into the space around you. Notice as you do this movement what happens.

9. Now, find the final reach through your arms into space. What do you notice? What changes in the constricted place in your body as you reach?

10. Connect with the center of your body by imagining and feeling into the area just below your navel.

11. Reach and extend your arms and imagine support coming from the center of your body. Then return the movement by going back to the center. Let that be a continuous sequence: reaching out and drawing back in. Repeat this movement and feel how it changes each time you do this. The slower you go, the more you will sense. What happens and what changes? Fill in the blanks:

    • When I extend into space, I notice _____.

    • When I return to center, I notice _____.

12. Repeat this movement until you feel a shift in the original constriction or you feel complete. Then stand quietly and observe what occurred as a shift within.

REFLECTION

In the space below or in your journal, respond to the following questions:

• What information do I have now about the constricted place in my body?

_____

_____

_____

• What does space have to offer me when I get tense?

_____

_____

_____

• What has been helpful to me in this exercise?

_____

_____

_____

Where Does My Attention Move?

PURPOSE

This simple practice helps you to sustain your own inner connection while you are working with clients. It is natural for a somatic movement therapist to resonate with and be impacted by clients' inner states, especially when moving with the client, holding sustained attention as they are exploring the disconnections in their body. This practice helps you re-engage your attention and presence, which are strongly needed as a guide. You will be moving through three distinct cycles of attention, each time having a slightly different focus to train your capacity to be with the somatic awareness of your attention.

INSTRUCTIONS

First-Cycle Attention

1. Let yourself notice your "first attention." Where is your immediate engagement with the client's somatic experience? Is it feeling the impact of their feelings or thinking about what you need to do next? Notice where your attention is on your client, and then relax and let go.

2. If you are sitting, root into your bones by feeling gravity and making any small adjustments so you can feel the contact with your seat. If you are standing, press your feet into the ground or make small shifts in your feet as if you are rooting them into the ground.

Second-Cycle Attention

3. Let yourself go inside and notice where your attention lands inside your own body. What is your experience in relation to the client?

4. Allow yourself to become more fluid by adding a small micro-movement. Loosen any tension or holding you might have. Engage subtle movement in your body.

Third-Cycle Attention

5. Notice your experience and practice staying with your inner experience, connecting with rooting and fluidity, even as you stay present with your client's experience. Notice if there is anything that gets in the way of being fully present.

6. Add a nuanced somatic breath by deepening your awareness into your roots and fluidity. Now, breathe with your whole body.

REFLECTION

Reflect on how the three cycles of attention move any stuck places within. What happens with the quality of your therapeutic connection as you complete this practice?

CHAPTER 11

SELF-TOUCH

*"The experience of movement and touch are basic to discovering who
we are and who is other and how we dance this life together."*

—**Bonnie Bainbridge Cohen**, *Sensing, Feeling and Action*

Touch and movement are intimately connected. As infants we are held and rocked in a loving embrace. Our early childhood experiences are through the senses—touching objects with our hands, feet, skin, and mouth is how we learn to recognize shapes and patterns. As we grow older, we continue to communicate and connect with others through touch and micro-expressions, more than any words could convey.

Movement is also how we learn to touch ourselves within. As you'll learn more in this chapter, the same brain regions are activated when we evaluate a moving object visually as when we touch the object with our hands. In other words, we can perceive touch through observation and action. This somatosensory information helps our nervous system to anticipate the textures of movements and touch.

When we open ourselves to perceiving the body as it is, and how it changes, we are connecting both the sensory and the motor activities in the brain. As Andrew Schwartz (2016) writes, "Cognitive neuroscience and systems neurophysiology are converging on the idea of movement as communication of intention from the brain to the external world" (p. 1131).

First Touch

"Touch is our most social sense."

—**Tiffany Field,** *Touch*

Our somatosensory system begins to develop prenatally in the seventh to eighth week of gestation. The first touch is water. The movement of the amniotic fluid within the womb stimulates sensitive nerve fibers known as C-tactile (CT) afferents, resulting in a calming effect on the embryo. After birth, these rhythmic motions remain preferred for soothing, calming, and reducing pain. Human caregivers intuitively rock and sway a newborn, providing soothing movements to help the baby grow and thrive. "Kangaroo care," in which the caregiver has prolonged skin-to-skin contact with the infant, has been shown to increase immune responses, decrease stress responses, and increase the survival rate of low-birthweight infants (Jefferies et al., 2012). Kangaroo care has been adopted as a standard care protocol for promoting human well-being and growth (WHO Immediate KMC Study Group et al., 2021).

Touch communication by the primary caregiver transmits on a somatic level that we are loved, we belong, and we are safe. Touch and emotions are intimately connected. Gentle touch can evoke feelings of closeness and the need for nurturing from others. Touch also affirms our personal boundaries; we learn to feel where we begin and end in relation to another.

Touch Receptors in the Body

"We carry a center that is always returning."

—Mark Nepo, *The Book of Awakening*

Our skin is the largest organ in the body of somatic perception. The skin has three layers—the dermis, epidermis, and hypodermis—which include touch receptors as part of our somatosensory system, a neural network that helps us to consciously perceive touch stimuli.

Touch comes in many forms, and our central nervous system can determine the pressure, location, duration, shape, movement, texture, vibration, and quality of touch. In the outermost epidermis layer (Meissner's corpuscles), we can detect motion on the skin. In the center dermis layer, we feel the stretching of our skin. At the border of the dermis and epidermis we can feel anything that is sharp and pointy on our skin. We feel the difference between firm and gentle pressure, heat and cold, and other touch qualities.

Through touch we receive information and transmit that stimulus through the skin and on to the central nervous system. A soothing touch can calm us; a rousing touch can bring energy to the body. Touch also engages various regions of the brain, such as the orbitofrontal cortex, which places a value on what we taste, hear, and see.

Oxytocin and natural opioids of the body are released during tactile stimulation, enhancing neuroplasticity changes in the brain. Novel tactile experiences open new neural sensory connections to facilitate more attention to embodiment.

What's really interesting is that we can initiate this same experience simply by *thinking* about being touched. Our sensitive CT fibers respond not only to actual physical contact, but also when we observe or imagine touch, such as being gently held or rocked. The mirror neuron system gets activated when we are imagining touch, which can lead to a reduction in anxiety and an increase in oxytocin, the bonding hormone (Chivukula et al., 2021). Touch connects us to the most innate resources of the body.

Relational Touch

"In the sweet territory of silence we touch the mystery."

—Angeles Arrien

When we receive touch, it is also linked with the facial expression of the toucher. These emotional micro-expressions are important—they are registered as the touch is delivered and encoded with an interpersonal feeling. Even if the therapist does not touch the client physically, the kind and warm face is a sort of touch to the client's inner experience. A kind, receptive face and voice can link to earlier memories of how touch was received in the past. When someone has not been touched with love and care, it has an impact on their sensory somatic felt sense; they can feel as if they don't belong to their body. Trauma often involves invasive or toxic touch, and trauma healing can bring a new sense of touch experience when done with care and ethical guidelines.

Many clients who have experienced interpersonal, attachment, or developmental trauma are sensitive to certain kinds of touch. Touch and movement can be powerful healing allies in helping the client recover a sense of innate wholeness. Movement can be a bridge toward building safety for therapeutic touch, as it is the first shape of touch way back in utero.

Guidelines for Working with Physical Touch

This chapter offers several exercises that are touch assisted. This means that you will provide touch—with clear boundaries—for the client so they can deepen their experience. Please note that the following guidelines must be met before offering touch to the client:

1. Discuss the use of touch and the ethics of touch. The code of ethics of the United States Association for Body Psychotherapy is a great resource (https://usabp.org/USABP-Code -of-Ethics).

2. The types of touch used in these exercises are to be done with consent and are nonsexual.

3. Explain the exercise to your client first and notice any hesitation. Do not proceed if the client is hesitant. Respect them not wanting to do the exercise without them having to explain why. Affirm their boundary; you can say, "Good that you know what is right for you. Thank you for letting me know."

4. Once the exercise is explained and they consent, only touch what is agreed. Do not move your hands on the body where touch has not been discussed. That can be very harmful to the client.

5. Ground yourself and affirm you own inner clear and clean boundaries when you touch.

6. Be mindful of the transitional moments when you approach the client's body's kinesphere and then when you leave it.

7. Be open, curious, and kind in your touch.

8. Remember that the touch is in support of the client's process.

Self-Touch

"Trust the opening and closing too; the expansion and the contraction; this is the heart's way of breathing."

—Jeff Foster, "How to Open Your Heart"

Another remarkable quality of our skin receptors is that we can distinguish between self-touch and being touched by others. In one study, researchers found that the brain reduces processing of sensory perception with self-touch (Boehme et al., 2019). This is not to say that self-touch is less effective than interpersonal touch, however. After all, when we bump into a sharp edge, we tend to rub the injured part of our body intuitively. When we are frightened, our first impulse is to bring a hand to rest over the heart region. These are movements toward the self. We touch to heal and soothe ourselves.

When we use touch with mindful awareness, we can harness this healing potential. Interpersonal touch can be complex, as it involves both the comfort level of the client being touched and the therapist being trained and comfortable touching ethically. Self-touch is accessible and fully within the client's control. It can provide immediate stress relief and regulate any activated body experience. When we move, we touch ourselves from the inside, and that builds internalized safety. I suggest using self-touch with movement to enhance the client's experience of self-care, self-regulation, and deeper awareness.

TIPS FOR SELF-TOUCH FOR CLIENTS

Share the following tips with your clients when you introduce self-touch practices:

- Listen to your body always. If something does not feel right, stop or change what you are practicing.
- Feel your own touch as if your hand is that of a kind and safe person.
- Bring kindness to your self-touch.
- Appreciate your capacity for self-care.
- See if you can include in movement some touch of your body that feels positive and affirming.
- See touch as a practice for meeting yourself.
- Listen to the hand touching and listen for the body being touched. How are the sensations different?

TIPS FOR THE THERAPIST INVITING SELF-TOUCH

The following are tips for you while guiding the client in self-touch. Be aware that inviting self-touch can be intimate and bring up shame.

- Touch evokes vulnerability and early memories, so be sensitive to that emerging.
- When you encourage self-touch, use invitational language such as "How about you touch your chest as you feel _____ [*note the emotion*]?"
- Respect when the client declines self-touch.
- Be sensitive to cultural differences; self-touch can be regarded differently from your assumptions, so be open and receptive.
- Self-touch can evoke negative feelings, so be prepared to process these as they arise.
- As you explore movement, you can invite your client to use self-touch. If it feels right, it can heighten and deepen the movement experience.
- Touch can be another movement felt through your skin. It can be a first embodied contact toward getting acquainted with the moving body. Self-touching and sensing one's breath underneath the touch is a felt experience of movement.

Diaphragm Breathing and Self-Touch

PURPOSE

This breath practice allows you to feel the rhythm of your own breathing. The diaphragm is an easy place to study the breath and feel both the fluidity and constriction of your breath.

INSTRUCTIONS

Hug your arms across your chest just beneath the armpits. Use a kind and loose hold, with your fingers resting on the sides of your rib cage, over your diaphragm.

1. Begin to sense into your breathing. Notice how your chest expands into your hands. Allow your breathing to slow down, moment by moment, and get curious about how the expansion widens your chest underneath your hands.

2. Can you receive your own touch? What happens as you pay attention to your breathing rhythm and the diaphragm expanding and contracting?

3. Now feel this breath as one continuous movement. What changes?

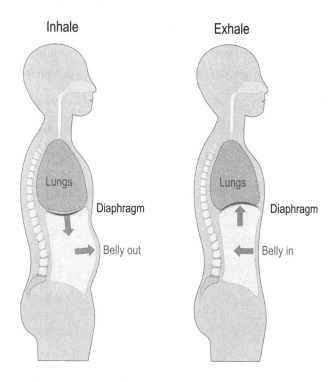

Self-Touch and Swaying

PURPOSE

This exercise is helpful when the client wants to soothe or calm an area in the body, such as tightness as a response to a traumatic memory. Self-touch will bring more awareness and sensation to the body. In this exercise, your client will use one area of the body to practice touch and movement. It is ideal to introduce this as a guided exercise. After practicing in session, you may want to assign it as homework.

INSTRUCTIONS

Once your client is comfortable with the basic structure of this exercise, you can invite them to expand to other areas of the body, when the client wants to do so. Ask the client to start standing, or adapt to sitting if needed. Guide them through the following script:

1. *Start by just noticing your body . . . now finish this sentence for me: "I feel _____."*

2. *Notice an area in the body that feels tight or activated, such as fast breath or frozenness. Fill in the blanks: "I feel _____ [tight, anxious, etc.] in my _____ [region of the body]."*

3. *Place one or both hands on the area you are noticing. Take a gentle breath and notice the touch. Fill in the blanks: "I feel _____ as I place my hand on _____. And the change I notice is _____."*

4. *Now bring a soft swaying motion as you continue to apply self-touch to that area on your body. Fill in the blanks: "I feel _____ under my hand and the movement is bringing me _____."*

5. *Stay with the touch and the swaying until you feel a shift or until you know it's not needed anymore.*

6. *Release the touch, pause your sway, and receive your body's sensations now.*

7. *Revisit in your attention the original area you started with and note the change. Fill in the blanks:*

   - *"The change I feel in my body is _____."*

   - *"I am now _____."*

   - *"Here are my other observations: _____."*

Across the Heart

PURPOSE

This exercise will help you to feel flow in the body. It's designed to move stuck energy in the body and at the same time bring emotion regulation through energizing, rhythmic movement. It combines self-touch with a focus on the chest region and heart.

INSTRUCTIONS

This is a sequential movement, meaning it's a more precise step-by-step motion. First learn the steps slowly, and then make this one continuous movement. The full movement is meant to be dynamic and coordinated with your inhale and exhale. However, listen to your body. If your body wants to rest along the movement path, then do that. The exercise can be done sitting or standing.

1. Sit or stand comfortably with your knees gently bent. Hold your head straight and keep your shoulders squared over your hips. Don't twist your body with this movement.

2. Bring your arms together, extended straight in front of your body, until your palms touch, keeping them comfortably at shoulder height. Again, as you move your arms, make sure you don't twist or rotate.

3. Begin to slide your right palm along your left inner arm, from the wrist to the armpit, at the same time as you extend your left arm out to the left side of your body, keeping it at shoulder height. As your left arm extends and your shoulder opens, it will create a natural path for your right palm to continue to slide toward the center of your chest, also known as the "heart center." You will end with your right hand over your heart center and your left arm still stretched out to the side, a bit like an archer with a drawn bow.

4. Pause with your right hand on your heart center for a moment.

5. Slide your right hand back across your left chest and along the inner left arm, which is at the same time moving to the front of you. Once you have brought both arms to the center in front of your body again, with your palms touching, pause for a moment.

6. Now you will repeat the previous three steps on the opposite side. Slide your left palm along your right inner arm, from the wrist to the armpit, while you extend your right arm out to the right side of your body, keeping it at shoulder height. Continue sliding your left palm toward your heart center while keeping your right arm stretched out to the side.

7. Pause with your left hand on your heart center for a moment.

8. Slide your left hand back across your right chest, along your inner right arm, which is at the same time moving to the front of you. Once both arms are centered in front of you again, palms touching, pause for a moment.

9. Repeat this full sequence (steps 3 through 8). Go slowly and get used to the motions.

10. On the third round, or when you feel comfortable doing so, coordinate your breath with the motions. Inhale as you bring your palm toward the heart center, hold briefly, and then exhale as you move the palm away from the heart center.

11. See if you can make this a flowing, smooth, continuous motion. Repeat the sequence another five to six times and then rest with your arms relaxed alongside your body. Or you can rest both hands on your chest over the heart center and sense into your heart.

VARIATION

Once you feel comfortable with the sequence, you can add bending and straightening your legs. Every time you are at the heart center, your legs are bent. When your hands are stretched out in front of you, your legs are straight. When coordinated with the breath, it becomes: inhale, slide to heart center, and bend; exhale, slide back, and straighten. This is a more vigorous motion, so do this only a few times, then notice the effect on your nervous system.

REFLECTION

In the space below or in your journal, respond to the following questions:

- What do you notice in your chest region?

  _____

  _____

- What is your overall body feeling?

  _____

  _____

- How would you rate your activation state right now, on a scale of 1 to 10 (with 10 being the most stressed)?

  _____

  _____

- What rhythm helped you the most?

  _____

  _____

CHAPTER 12

DEVELOPMENTAL MOVEMENTS AND EXTENDING AWARENESS

"There is a sense of wonderment as the mover's hands discover and explore the shape of his or her own body. As the mover's hands shape themselves to the bulges and the hollows, the hard bones and the soft flesh, there is a profound sense of self-recognition—as if meeting oneself for the first time."

—**Joan Chodorow,** *"The Body as Symbol"*

We all discover our bodies, our relationships, and the world around us as we mature on our human developmental journey. Developmental movements are our body's way of learning how to perceive the world. Through our first five years, our developmental movement patterns guide us through self-perception, self-knowing, and relational discovery. We learn to move, crawl, walk, stand, orient our spatial awareness, and assert our place in our human family.

As mentioned in earlier chapters, every interaction the infant has and how they are responded to creates a balance and rhythm of relationship that gets internalized. If the infant reaches out and is met with a loving gaze, a reach back, and gentle touch, the message that gets internalized is that of affirmation, love, and support. The infant learns that this reach is worth doing and will be rewarded. If the caregiver is inattentive, depressed, anxious, or otherwise unable to provide that loving, soothing feedback, the messages will be different and can result in the infant giving up, contracting, or becoming frustrated. If these emotions are not regulated, the infant can become distressed and confused about their inner somatic signals.

When we have experienced trauma in the first six months of our life, our development is impacted neurologically, which can have a constricting impact on our movement capacity. During this sensitive infancy time, we learn how to yield weight, grasp without fear, reach out to others and be reached for, and experience safety in another. When trauma immobility is interfering with these developmental needs, somatic patterns begin to emerge. These often become assumed personality traits rather than stuck trauma movement responses.

We sense our world through the direct experience of our body. Over time, we learn to embody what we sense, feel, and think into beliefs, which become the foundation of how we navigate our inner and outer worlds. Our sense of self, our somatic knowledge within, is based on what our experiences have been.

Safety, well-being, connection, creativity, self-confidence, and many more qualities emerge depending on our experiences. We organize our perceptions, beliefs, and behaviors based on our lived experience.

Re-patterning

"Movement is one of the most direct ways to reach back to our earliest experiences."
—**Joan Chodorow,** "The Body as Symbol"

Fortunately, we can gently learn about our developmental impact by mindfully moving through certain states to re-pattern our nervous system and the learned emotional beliefs associated with it. For example, a sense of falling and not being supported as an infant can be a lifelong theme in believing that the world is not trustworthy. By consciously moving this developmental state, your client can learn about this imprint and create new possibilities for somatic healing.

In session, this dynamic of early relational qualities can be intentionally worked on with physical distance and closeness. The physical distance between client and therapist is both an assessment tool and an intervention. Gauging how far or near the client wants to be to us, we can learn of the client's need for safety, closeness, and distance. As somatic movement therapists, we are sensitive to the reaching the client does or doesn't do. These primal movement patterns of reaching for someone or yearning for being reached toward can be a helpful tool as we work with the attachment wounds of developmental trauma.

First Connection

After birth, ideally the infant is placed on the mother's body to begin the bonding process. The infant yields its weight onto the surface of the mother's body into warmth and safety. The infant rests and releases into the caregiver, breathing in reciprocity. This basic motif of breathing with someone else is a deep somatic experience of being met. We are being breathed with and received in the entirety of our body. Your client can explore this in the *Yielding* exercise in this chapter.

When we are held, rocked, and nurtured through loving touch, we are receiving a deep message of being cared for into our body in a very direct way. When our caregiver is stressed, anxious, or not embodied, we can't experience the sense of yielding into safety.

There is a lasting relationship between one's internal rhythm and organicity and the quality of one's yielding capacity. When there is anxiety in the body, the weight can't be fully released, and the sensation of yielding is not complete. Trusting one's weight into the earth is a basic trust into beingness.

This idea of connection with the earth can be explored, particularly when themes of not feeling connected or grounded come up for your client. The exercise *Grounding Through Navel Radiation* is designed for just that. Every mammal has a variation of bringing their belly to the ground to rest, recuperate, and connect back into themselves. This primal impulse can be appreciated as a type of umbilical cord, connecting us with our mother's placenta for nourishment and connection. The navel is deeply rooted and allows the infant to lift their head up to discover the world. It is like an anchor rooted into the earth. At some point, you may need to invite your client back into a primal connection with the earth.

Offering Developmental Movements in Your Client

The exercises in this chapter are a safe way to explore the internal signals to heal developmental trauma. Make sure you go slowly and mindfully, and explore what is occurring and what wants to happen. Be fully present as the client explores developmental movements such as yielding and reaching. Make sure you gently encourage them and provide safety and care.

The client might drop into sensitivity and neediness. They might ask you to come closer or to answer the reaching they are doing. My suggestion is to stay in your professional comfort zone above all, and then gauge what is therapeutically needed. If the client has a missing experience of needing another to reach back to them, you can set this exploration up with mindfulness. For example, you can say: "I will reach back to you, and you study what comes up for you." If you frame this as an exploration for the client to study, you will minimize the transference and the confusion that might happen for the client. It gives you a very defined and clear role in the experiment. Because boundaries have often been violated at this age of development, being clear and precise and naming your role is essential. You can then follow up after you finish the exercise by asking: "What was that like when you reached and then I answered the reach? Who was that person you reached toward, that I stood in for?" This will bring the exploration into the therapeutic frame and encourage the client to take responsibility for their movement experience.

When you debrief a movement exercise on the floor, make sure you bring a little bit of physical distance, indicating that you are shifting from exploration to alignment and processing about it. Again, you are working with subtle boundary settings. You can also shift back into the chairs and talk about the experience from the more adult state rather than the infant state they might have explored.

Yielding

PURPOSE

Feeling one's weight into the earth is a basic form of trust into beingness. In this exercise, you are helping your client restore their basic relationship with yielding to and trusting gravity. There is a deep relationship between one's internal rhythm and organicity and the quality of one's yielding capacity.

It is ideal to introduce this as a guided exercise. After practicing in session, you may want to assign it as homework.

INSTRUCTIONS

This exercise is best done lying on the belly. Have your client support their face and neck by having their hands stacked underneath their forehead or using a towel or pillow. Their head can be sideways; just make sure their neck is comfortable and that their breathing is not obstructed. The surface needs to be comfortable, not too soft and not too firm. Have a couple of blankets handy.

As they do this exercise, it can help if they imagine an infant resting on the earth (or on a caregiver) and releasing into gravity. Encourage them to imagine a positive relationship, with the caregiver breathing in and out, receiving and affirming the weight of the infant. Say:

1. *Let your belly rest on the floor. Let your legs be relaxed and rotate them outward so that the front of your pelvis is in contact with the ground. You can cover yourself with a blanket if you like.*

2. *As you assume this body posture, sense your weight into the earth. Allow gravity to invite you.*

3. *Feel your breath go smoothly in and out, and feel the slight pressure when you inhale with your belly against the ground.*

4. *With each breathing cycle, soften your belly into the ground. Imagine that your belly becomes wider and sinks into the soft ground . . . imagine the earth being warm and inviting and waiting for you to release into it.*

5. *As you breathe slowly, remember these simple words: "I am breath, I am movement, I am life." You can simply remember these words, say them to yourself, or have me speak them to you. Notice what your body sensations and feelings are as you hear these words.*

6. *Imagine that the earth is breathing you in as you exhale, and that the earth is giving you life as you inhale. Take your time and notice the rhythm of the yielding sensations that are subtly occurring. You don't have to "do" anything; let the movement of yielding simply happen . . . notice what softens in your body as you yield.*

7. *What kind of subtle motions are you aware of now? Take your time—you will know when it is enough. Your body will want to move, to shift posture . . . go ahead and let that happen. You might rest on your side or lie on your back, staying with your body.*

8. *When you are ready, sit up and reflect.*

REFLECTION

Invite your client to journal their responses to the following questions:

- What is the yielding movement bringing you?

- How do you know you are in connection with the earth or support?

- How would you describe your internal state after this exercise?

Spinal Rolling

PURPOSE

This exercise will bring somatic awareness to the spine. The spine is an important core organizer in our posture and how we hold ourselves up. When we are under threat, the spine can stiffen and get stuck in holding tension chronically. You can assess how far the client is able and willing to go with this exercise. The objective is not to push the body but to encourage a sense of fluidity in the spine and back.

TIPS

Many clients struggle with the effort of wanting to get somewhere. See if you can ease this ambition and invite a gradual sensing of rolling down with gravity and rolling back up slowly. You can work with images that represent how the spine can be fluid, such as pearl strands or seaweed moving in water, or ask the client to come up with their own image. It is ideal to introduce this as a guided exercise. After practicing in session, you may want to assign it as homework.

INSTRUCTIONS

Introduce the concept of gravity and allowing the body to roll down with that gentle force. As the client rolls back up, have them use their pelvis as an anchor against gravity. Use the following script.

Posture and Intention

1. *Take a wide standing position with your feet slightly wider than your hips. Make sure your feet are parallel.*

2. *Visualize your spine as you are standing. Feel the extension to the sky and to the earth, and how your spine is in between.*

3. *Set the intention that this is not a stretching exercise. There is no goal to get anywhere. We will simply explore the relationship with gravity.*

Rolling Down

4. *Slowly begin to bow your head forward and let the weight of your head initiate the movement of rolling downward. Take your time and go very slowly. Let your arms hang alongside your body and follow the natural progression of the movement unfolding.*

5. *Let your head be invited by gravity and now begin to connect with the vertebrae of your spine. See if you can feel each one of them by slowly breathing into your spine.*

6. *If there is an area that is stiff or held, pause and breathe. If there is pain, back up and ease the movement into a range that is accessible to you.*

7. *Let your knees be soft and with a gentle bend.*

8. *At any time, you can pause and sense into your spine and allow for any lateral movements, such as gentle swaying. Make these movements small and mindful so you can stay connected with your spine.*

9. *Go as far as your body wants to without strain.*

Rolling Up

10. *When you are at the point where you feel you want to return, again connect with your intention to feel your spine as a support.*

11. *Ground your feet into the earth. Feel your pelvis as a heavy weight that reaches toward the ground.*

12. *Let the pressure into the earth initiate the rolling-up movement. Go very slowly—this is an important transition moment. Roll your spine up as slowly as you went down. Feel every vertebra. Even if you skip some or it feels clunky, sense into your spine as a fluid unfolding process. Roll up slowly, letting your arms dangle and fall into place on their own . . . let your neck and head be the very last to straighten.*

Standing Receiving the Somatic Messages

13. *Stand still now, and close your eyes if that feels comfortable for you.*

14. *Sense into your whole spine:*

    • *What sensations are present?*

    • *How do you experience your spine now?*

    • *If your spine could give you a message, what would that be?*

REFLECTION

Discuss or invite your client to journal their responses to the following questions:

• What messages did you receive from your body during this exercise?

• How does the spinal rolling help you with your trauma responses?

• Do you feel more grounded, spacious, centered?

• What does the spine represent for you?

Belly Earth Resting

PURPOSE

This is a deeply restorative, passive movement to use when the client experiences overwhelm, shutdown, or emotional confusion. This practice can teach a restorative connection between the center of the body and the earth.

INSTRUCTIONS

To set up a comfortable space for this exercise, make sure to have a soft surface available, plus blankets and pillows. The body can cool during this exercise, so use one of the blankets to cover the client if needed. Use a calm, gentle voice to guide the client into a deep restful state. Allow the posture to do the work for the client.

Ask the client to lie down with their belly to the ground. Their legs should be stretched long and wide enough so that ideally the hips are opened and in complete contact with the ground. The insides of the legs and the inner sides of the feet will also be touching the ground. The client can turn their face to one side or place a pillow beneath their forehead so that the neck is not strained. Take time to help your client find a comfortable position, since they will be in this pose for five to seven minutes. Then guide them through the following script:

1. *Start by feeling the body position and make sure there is no strain anywhere. Then fully relax into this posture. Feel held by the ground beneath you . . . there is nothing you need to do, nothing you need to move right now.*

2. *Feel the pressure of your breath against the floor, and allow your breath to slow down . . . notice how the breath is its own movement—you don't have to do anything. Your body is moving you. It's okay to rest now.*

3. *Receive the body as it is right now . . . be still and sense. Take your time and deeply listen to your soma. Receive the body as it is right now . . . [repeat a few more times as needed until the client's breath slows].*

4. After five to seven minutes, slowly transition. Invite the client to roll to the side of their body. Have them pause and then sit up slowly.

REFLECTION

Discuss the experience. Ask your client to describe what is happening inside right now.

Push and No

PURPOSE

In this exercise you will help your client explore the internal impulse for a "no." A push is a physical movement for no. Here your client can mindfully explore both the internal and external movement for no.

INSTRUCTIONS

Use the following script to guide your client:

1. *Start by feeling in your body where there is a "no." It can be toward a person, a situation, or a feeling in the body.*

2. *Now connect with your hands and arms, and extend them forward, making a pushing movement.*

3. *Feel into what that movement does inside and to the no you feel. Does it get stronger? Is there a conflict? Is there a doubt? What could support the push right now?*

4. *Repeat the movement until you feel clarity.*

REFLECTION

In their journal, have the client respond to the following prompt: "When I feel an inner no and push, I experience _____."

Reach and Yes

PURPOSE

This exercise explores the impulse to reach for and connect with what we want, whether a person, object, or goal. This reaching motion is an early developmental task as well as a continued movement we do with others. It can bring many aspects into the client's awareness, including an ambivalence toward wanting to reach out and receive contact.

TIPS

If the client is reaching toward you, make sure you clarify the role you are occupying. Discuss any potential transference here, especially in light of the client's attachment relationships. For example, they may want you to stand in for their parents. In this case, start with the client reaching toward an object, then clarify the person the client is reaching toward and study the feelings that come up. When you then step into that role, say: "I am stepping into the role as your parent for you to study your reach." Notice what happens. In the debrief, clarify any confusion or transference the client might have.

INSTRUCTIONS

Have an empty chair, pillow, or other object available for the client to reach toward. The client can be in a seated or standing position. Guide them through the following script.

Neutral Reach

1. *Start with a neutral reach, meaning that you use the reaching motion without any imagination or memory. Just follow the first impulse that comes to you when you think of reaching.*

2. *Notice what it evokes as you explore the movement of reaching.*

3. *Fill in the blanks aloud: "When I reach, I feel _____. When I reach, I remember _____."*

Object Reach

4. *Now imagine reaching toward someone. This might be a person in your past, such as a caregiver. Imagine they are sitting on the [chair/pillow]. Imagine reaching for them.*

5. *Notice what happens in your hands and arms. Do they feel excited and want to move? Where does the impulse to reach start? Or is there a holding back? Where do you notice that barrier?*

6. *Now use your arms to reach toward them and as you do, notice what comes up:*

    - *Are you anticipating a welcome or a rejection?*

    - *How is the rest of your body responding right now?*

    - *What did you start believing about reaching out for others?*

7. *Take a rest. Feel your body and reflect on what came up.*

Therapist Reach

8. *In this next cycle, you will reach toward me. I'm a stand-in for the person that you want to reach toward and want a response from.*

9. *Reach toward me. Notice when I stay neutral. What happens to your reach? Fill in the blank: "I feel _____."*

10. *Now reach toward me again.* [As the client reaches toward you, reach your arm toward them as if welcoming them. Be mindful, intentional, and neutral. Hold the reach so that the client can notice the subtleties of this movement of reaching toward each other.] *Notice how this feels:*

    - *What comes up?*

    - *Do you feel a yes inside?*

    - *Do you feel ambivalence, worry, or fear come up?*

REFLECTION

After a rest, reflect on what came up for the client either by discussing or journaling.

Grasp and Pull Toward

PURPOSE

In this exercise, you are inviting the client to explore another early developmental movement: the grasping response. Grasping is used to hold on to another person, to ensure safety by clinging to their body, to bring them closer. In this exploration, your client can learn about the need for safety and close contact as well as the fear of disconnection.

INSTRUCTIONS

This exercise can be done sitting or standing. Use a rope, towel, scarf, or anything that can withstand some pressure. Place one end in your hands and the other end in the client's hands.

First Cycle

1. Take a moment together to feel the holding of the rope.

2. Ask the client to tug on the rope. You should not respond to the tug.

3. Ask the client, *What is the next impulse and feeling in your body as you receive this response? . . . Follow that impulse and do whatever movement comes with it.*

Second Cycle

4. Ask the client to tug again. This time, respond by tugging back.

5. Ask the client, *What is the next impulse and feeling in your body as you receive this response? . . . Follow that impulse and whatever movement comes with it.*

Third Cycle

6. In this last round, initiate a tug yourself. Notice what happens.

7. Ask your client, *What is the next impulse and feeling in your body as you receive this response? . . . Follow that impulse and whatever movement comes with it.*

REFLECTION

Discuss what these movement dynamics are telling the client right now.

Five-Movement Sequence

PURPOSE

This exercise is about helping your client discover their intuitive developmental movements: yielding, pushing, reaching, grasping, and pulling. These five movements are part of the relational repertoire when first engaging with our primary caregivers. In exploring these qualities, we can learn what has felt supportive and what has not been met. Your client can discover how it felt inside then and how it feels now as they engage mindfully with the five movement qualities.

TIPS

It can be helpful to repeat the cycle a couple of times, once for the client to get used to the movements and again to study what your client is noticing inside while doing these motions. Remember to stay neutral and coach the client into noticing the movement and the effect it has inside.

INSTRUCTIONS

Move the client through these five movement qualities mindfully and sequentially. Note which movements come with ease and play, and which ones feel more challenging. Invite your client to do the same. The final step in the process involves resting and integrating all five qualities.

Your client can do these movements sitting or standing. The exploration of grasp and pull will involve an object such as a rope, scarf, or towel. Use the following script to guide them.

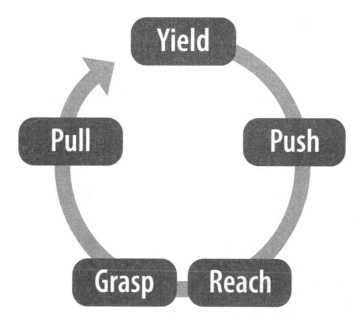

Introduction

1. Let yourself be intuitive and mindful in this exercise. You might notice different feelings, body memories, or pauses with the movement qualities. You are welcome to keep your journal handy and write down what you are sensing in your body as we go.

2. We will be exploring five human development qualities: yielding, pushing, reaching, grasping, and pulling. These qualities are in a cyclical relationship with each other. Study them with an open mind and see what comes up. We will track which movements might have a settling emotional tone to them and seem more evocative, so we can understand more deeply the relational thematic patterns you are experiencing.

3. If at any time a movement feels overwhelming, you can stop and return to a movement that is more resourcing for you.

Yield

4. We will start with the movement quality of yielding. Think of it as a resource, support, or grounding. Infants yield when they are held and supported by a loving caregiver. You can tune into the support that the earth and gravity provide for you. That support is here for you, without your having to do anything.

5. Sit or lie down, and let your body be supported by the ground or the chair holding your body. Relax the muscles in your body and see if you can breathe into any tightness, bracing, or holding. See if you can let your body be held.

6. Notice what arises in this non-moving, non-striving action of receiving.

7. Fill in these blanks for me, either out loud or in your journal, if it feels more supportive:
    *   "When I yield, I sense my body _____."
    *   "I yield and I want to move in this way: _____."

Push

8. Now bring awareness to your feet, toes, fingers, and hands. Bring an impulse to these areas to initiate a push motion. Start simply and study what comes up.

9. You can push with a person across from you in mind. This is just to have a target and not about the other person. You can also push without any person or target.

10. Feel and sense into the action of pushing . . . get acquainted with what pushing in your body feels like and what follows a push motion.

11. Fill in the blanks out loud or in your journal:
    *   "When I push, I sense _____."
    *   "When I push, I feel _____."
    *   "I push from this place in my body: _____."

- *"When I push, I want to follow that by moving like _____."*
- *"When I push, I want _____."*

Reach

12. *Now we will explore reaching. Start with one hand and open the palm of the hand.*

13. *With the open hand, point toward someone or something you are working with.*

14. *Now move the open hand as if reaching toward the person or object. Extend your arm until it reaches a natural resting position and hold that position.*

15. *Notice what comes up. Are you reaching from your fingers, your hand, or a deeper place inside? What is the next impulse that wants to follow?*

16. *Fill in these blanks, either out loud or in your journal:*
    - *"When I reach, I sense _____."*
    - *"When I reach, I feel _____."*
    - *"I reach from this place in my body: _____."*
    - *"When I reach, I want to follow that by moving like _____."*
    - *"When I reach, I want _____."*

Grasp

17. [For this movement, you will need a rope, scarf, or towel. Place it between you and the client, each of you holding one end. Then gently tug on it so that the client can study their own grasp impulse.]

18. *When you feel a tug on the other side of the* [rope/scarf/towel], *notice your impulse. Do you want to hold tighter or let go?*

19. [Repeat this movement a couple of times, altering the speed and strength of the grasps.]
    - *What feeling comes up with that?*
    - *What is the next impulse that arises?*

20. *Fill in the blanks, either out loud or in your journal:*
    - *"When I grasp, I sense _____."*
    - *"When I grasp, I feel _____."*
    - *"I grasp from this place in my body: _____."*
    - *"When I grasp, I want to follow that by moving like _____."*
    - *"When I grasp, I want _____."*

Pull

21. [Keep using the rope, scarf, or towel for this movement. If that is too provocative, you can have your client use a pulling motion without the resistance of you offering the pulling back.]

22. *Pull with one or both hands. Notice how you are doing that. Are you clenching your fists? Using a downward movement? Pulling from the whole arm or whole body? What kind of effort is here?*

23. *Fill in the blanks, either out loud or in your journal:*
    - *"When I pull, I sense _____."*
    - *"When I pull, I feel _____."*
    - *"I pull from this place in my body: _____."*
    - *"When I pull, I want to follow that by moving like _____."*
    - *"When I pull, I want _____."*

Return to Yield and Rest

24. *Now let your movement rest into yielding again. Feel the support of the* [floor/chair/couch]. *Simply rest into doing nothing. Notice what movement was most intriguing for you.*

Grounding Through Navel Radiation

PURPOSE

This simple exercise is designed to help the client reconnect with deep impulses in the body and foster a sense of direct connection with the earth and their navel center. It can be very helpful when your client is not feeling connected or grounded. It is both a restful and active movement.

The connection with our navel is an ancient movement pattern that began in utero with our umbilical connection. We develop agency of our limbs from the center out and receive proprioceptive feedback from the limbs and skin back into our navel center. In this guided exercise, the goal is for your client to feel a connection with the earth as a sustaining energy from which to initiate movement into the world. This is a developmental movement infants do when they are fully supported by the ground and are curious about the world. Once the infant feels that connection of their navel with the floor, they can lift their head and engage their arms, hands, legs, and feet to discover their surroundings. Trauma can truncate the impulse to discover; here the client can restore that first impulse to connect.

INSTRUCTIONS

Guide your client through the following script:

1. *Lie down on the ground face down. You can support your head with your hands, keeping your head and neck straight. Let your belly rest on the ground and rotate your legs out so your pelvis is in contact with the ground.*

2. *Take three deep belly breaths, feeling the pressure in your belly when breathing in and feeling it soften when breathing out.*

3. *Focus now on your navel, the center of your body. Let your breath come in and out as if you are breathing through the navel itself.*

4. *Connect deeply with the earth beneath you through the navel breathing. Root into your navel as an anchor. Feel the support and feel any impulse of wanting to explore. The body is not passively receiving; it is active.*

5. *Begin to bring a small motion to the navel as you breathe. The breath itself can be a movement, or you can begin to wiggle and shimmy around your belly button. Use your navel as a stabilizer, rooting into the ground.*

6. *Begin to lift your head up and down from the navel awareness and notice how you are feeling connected from the center of your body as you move. Feel how the lift of your head connects all the way to that center in your belly. Feel the impulse to connect outwardly.*

7. *Let this motion from the navel radiate out, as the seat and organ of your moving body. Imagine being a starfish radiating out from the navel center.*

8. *Now engage your feet. Curl your toes under and feel the power through your legs and to your navel. Give your toes a little push into the ground. Notice the quality of movement that is happening right now.*

9. *How do you perceive your body from this rooted navel position? What are the movements that want to follow now? What are you curious about?*

10. *Keep your head lifted and connected to your navel at the same time. Notice what motions are wanting to happen. Push your hands into the ground as you push your toes and feet into the ground. Can you feel a charge moving through them and into your belly?*

11. *Follow any movement that wants to happen right now. Are there any surges of power or energy coming forth? How can you support the movements that want to come forth?*

12. *Now rest your entire body on the ground and sense into what is now in the navel area.*

13. *Roll to one side, then sit up. As you shift your posture, notice your connection to your center. In the seated position, check in with your body and how much activity or impulse to move is here.*

REFLECTION

Discuss aloud or have your client journal in response to the following questions:

- How does my connection with the navel and ground affect my being centered?

- How do I lose contact with my center? How do I return to my center?

- When I connect with my navel motions, what qualities come up?

- What kind of action can I feel when I am supported in my center?

- How can I bring this navel-center connection into my daily life?

Arching Motions

PURPOSE

This exercise is helpful if you see spontaneous arching movement in the client as they discover developmental trauma or shock trauma. This is a common movement pattern in response to an overwhelming event—we arch our back as if we are stunned or shocked. It can be an early startle response that is being relived in the body. When you see this arching movement, you can help your client to sensitively work through it.

INSTRUCTIONS

It is important to go very slowly and have the client be in control of their movements. Stop frequently as you sequence this movement and find the places in the body that want to integrate. Allow time for the client to become conscious of this movement pattern and then find a resolution. Make sure they do not get stuck in that motion.

For sensitive areas such as the neck, offer a pillow for support if needed. Also ensure the client has a writing utensil and their journal or other paper to draw on.

If you see an arching movement, you will likely see it in the neck or upper back, as if the client is extending themselves away.

1. First, bring awareness to the arching movement. You can say, *Let's notice together this movement you just did. I saw you arching backward.* Mirror their motion very slowly and ask, *Are you curious to explore this?*

2. Say, *Go ahead and repeat the movement now, but slow it way, way down so you can feel it more consciously.*

3. Discover the pathway of arching and what it is doing inside. Say, *"As you feel this arching pathway in your* [body, neck, back, etc.]*, what are you discovering in that movement?"*

4. Pause. Invite your client to come to a neutral position and notice what is happening. Process together if needed.

5. Continue to explore the movement and then take more time to process with your client what comes up. You might ask, *What did this movement do—how did it serve you?*

6. Invite your client to draw what has changed in the arching movement.

Extending Planes of Awareness

PURPOSE

This is a grounding and orienting exercise to help the client feel their body in relation with the planes of physical space awareness. We can find our center when we learn to extend our awareness into our environment. With many relational or collective traumas, the client can feel as if the space around them is small or there is no room for them; as a result, they may collapse into themselves. This is a supportive practice when the client wants to take up space and reestablish body boundaries. The here-and-now awareness of their physical presence in space can help them to reclaim a sense of self-agency.

INSTRUCTIONS

Guide your client through the following script:

1. *Start in a comfortable standing position. Let your body be neutral and place your attention within. Throughout this exercise, notice how your presence and embodiment changes as you follow the movement sequences. Move your physical body around the different planes to feel the space you are taking up.*

2. *Feel your standing posture and lift through your head toward an upright but relaxed position. Have your arms resting at your sides.*

3. *Begin to turn your head slowly and deliberately from side to side, orienting in the space around you . . . then return to center, facing in front of you, and take a breath.*

4. *Notice the space in front of you and behind you. Lift your arms in front of you as if to describe or outline the front plane that extends ahead of you . . . and then move your arms slightly behind your body as if to illustrate the back plane behind your body. Become aware of the front and back planes in which your body is the center. Then relax your arms, take a breath, and notice your experience.*

5. *Now become aware of the vertical space around you. Reach your arms above your head as if you're reaching up toward the sky and take a breath . . . then reach down toward the ground, taking another breath. Notice your experience as you relax your arms alongside your body. Feel the horizontal and vertical awareness in which your body is the center.*

6. *Now bring your attention to the horizontal space to the left and right sides of your body. You can extend your arms sideways, reaching away from your body, and then slight rotation as if drawing a large circle around your body . . . then let your arms relax at your sides, take a deep breath, and feel the horizontal plane in which your body is the center.*

7. *Begin now to move and walk through the space around you while maintaining your awareness of the vertical and horizontal planes all at the same time. What happens with your sense of connection with the immediate environment as you inhabit all these planes of awareness?*

8. *As you continue to walk and move around, inhabiting these planes of awareness, notice what happens with your embodiment. How would you describe it?*

9. *Now come to a neutral position . . . relax and simply notice how your body feels after this exercise.*

CHAPTER 13

BREATH, SOUND, AND INTRINSIC MOVEMENT

"Sound moves molecules and organic material, including the tissues of our body, changing densities to create more space and permeability."
—**Robert Litman,** *The Breathable Body*

Sounds are of primordial nature; we are all capable of making sounds and they can be deeply healing. Breath and sounds often go together, and you can invite your client to experiment with making breath sounds, or *sounding*, and then have them notice how their breathing rhythm changes. Sounds and conscious breathing are a powerful way to shift inner states. They can be very calming or energizing. Of course, with any of these movements you want to track for any activation and observe if any of the breaths or sounds are too much for the client.

Sounds transmit into the ear through a sequence of vibrations. We can think of these as small movements that are traveling into the brain through the vestibular system. The signals of the sound are received by the vestibulocochlear nerve and processed in the brain. Both the amygdala and hippocampus receive sensory information from the auditory system and are affected by sound. This is critical in trauma healing, as these two regions of the brain are impacted by trauma experiences.

Music and sounds can lift our mood and alleviate our negative mind states. They help to downregulate stress responses and can induce the parasympathetic rest and digest response. In trauma healing, sounds, breath, and movement combined can have a deep impact on the somatic and autonomic nervous systems (Bartel & Mosabbir, 2021). Sound vibrations are considered a stimulus, and the rhythmic effect of sound and movement stimulates cellular activity and initiates a neural modulation response. Making sounds is a playful, psychospiritual activity that has been used in healing techniques since ancient times (Goldsby & Goldsby, 2020). Recently, there has been a resurgence of sound healing, a practice the ancient Greeks used to treat mental health (Landis-Shack et al., 2017).

Using Therapeutic Sound and Breath

Both breath and sound can enhance the feelings and sensations of the body and can bring up fear, awkwardness, or shame. Making a sound can relate to trauma states, and conscious breathing can bring up resistance and internal barriers to feeling. Therefore, it is important to be mindful of how you introduce sounds and breathing with the client.

Fight or flight responses bring more breath intake and a faster rhythm; most people breathe through the mouth when these responses are triggered. Clients can begin to take in too much breath and become lightheaded, dizzy, or panicky. The tendency is to tighten and stiffen their body in response. Introducing a gentle movement—such as swaying, rocking, or walking—can ease that constriction in the body. Encourage slow breathing through the nose.

Be sensitive to the discomfort or shyness that might come along with this type of work. Sounding is a way to affirm one's presence and it can be challenging at first. Offering to sound with the client is very helpful. I often begin with breath awareness (see the *5-5-8 Sensate Breathing* exercise), especially with clients who feel worried about working with their sensations.

Here are some additional tips for introducing the use of therapeutic sound:

- Explain the reason for using the sound.

- Introduce sound as a natural way our bodies express.

- Keep in mind that sound is a form of intrinsic movement practice and can make larger movements more accessible.

- Encourage the exploration of both sound and breath, since they are related.

- Encourage the client to playfully make sounds that feel good in their body.

- If feelings of resistance come up, be patient, alter the exercise to make it more accessible to the client, or pause and process what is coming up in response.

Here are further tips for introducing the use of therapeutic breath:

- When fight or flight responses are triggered, introduce slow nose breathing. This will induce the ventral vagal rest and digest response.

- When there is a trigger, encourage gentle movements in the body; swaying and rocking are helpful motions.

- Encourage mindful breathing, being present with the sensations of breathing and the impact of the breath on the whole body. This is empowering, as the client has self-agency over changing their internal state through their breathing.

5-5-8 Sensate Breathing

PURPOSE

This is a very easy way to get your client to start familiarizing themselves with their inhale and exhale. This simple counting technique will help them to get used to observing sensations and to become more curious and open to further exploration.

INSTRUCTIONS

1. *Cast your eyes down or close them, if that feels comfortable for you.*

2. *Notice your breath. On your next inhale, breathe in slowly through your nose to the count of 5 . . . then exhale slowly to the count of 5. Or, if you discover that you want to inhale for 5 and exhale for 8, go ahead and let that happen.*

3. *Allow this rhythm to continue until you feel you are comfortable. Listen to your body as you explore this breath.*

4. *When you feel you have the rhythm, drop the counting and continue breathing slowly in and out. Trust your breath without the counting. Take slow, deliberate inhales and exhales . . . feel the fluidity of the breath as it starts in the back of your lungs, slowly fills your chest and nose, then gently releases. Focus on any sensations that you are curious about.*

REFLECTION

Discuss what the experience was like. Pose the following questions to your client:

- What kind of sensations do you notice at your nostrils as you inhale?
- What happens as you exhale? Are the sensations different?
- What do you become aware of in your chest region?
- What happens with your thoughts and mental activity?
- Where are the most dominant sensations in your body?
- What do you feel about these sensations now?
- What is it like to breathe from the back of your lungs and relax into your own breathing rhythm?

Ahh's and Ohh's

PURPOSE

Ahh and *ohh* are both primordial sounds that can open different areas of the body to increase sensation and awareness. It is ideal to introduce this as a guided exercise. After practicing in session, you may want to assign it as homework.

INSTRUCTIONS

Tell your client that when they're working with sound and breath, they want to bring together awareness of both, so they can feel the breath and the sound and the sound and the breath. This focused attention will help to regulate their nervous system.

It can be helpful to model this sound and breath practice for the client first. As you are modeling, you want to avoid being performative. Rather, enjoy and be with the moment-to-moment unfolding of these sound breaths.

Guide your client through the following script:

1. *Take a soft, long inhale and then, on your exhale, gently open your mouth and let the sound and the breath come out as one long, sustained* **ahh***. Follow the sound until the exhale is fully completed.*

2. *Take a moment and rest in hearing the aftermath of the sound.*

3. *Then take in another soft, long inhale and exhale with another* **ahh** *sound. Repeat this three times.*

4. *Now let's switch to the* **ohh** *sound. Take a long, soft inhale, gently open your mouth, and allow a low-frequency* **ohh** *sound to accompany the exhale. Listen to the sound as you're making it.*

5. *As you finish the sound and breath, rest and enjoy a moment of stillness.*

6. *Then repeat the* **ohh** *sound three times.*

7. *Now alternate the* **ahh** *sound and the* **ohh** *sound, taking your time and listening to each moment of the sound-breath and how it affects your body. Stay relaxed and enjoy the sound-breath until you find a natural completion.*

REFLECTION

Discuss how your client's body and mind feel after this exercise.

Vu Sound

PURPOSE

The *vu* sound was developed by Continuum teacher Susan Harper, who wanted to provide a sound that felt safe and nourishing to the nervous system. The vu sound brings your client back into connection with the primal energy of life and love. It has a low frequency that can be felt palpably through the body. This breath will help to ground and settle the nervous system and can be used to regulate. It can also be used to bring the client more in touch with their body.

TIPS

As you introduce this sound, you can bring forth images of light, warmth, radiance, and inner brightness.

INSTRUCTIONS

When working with the vu sound, model it first. Then have the client try it to see if they have the mechanics of the sound. Clients are often very self-conscious about making sounds and looking "funny." Since this is a sound that involves visibly pursed lips, you want to normalize this for the client by either doing it first or doing it together. Guide them through the following script.

Before the Sound

1. *Before we begin, notice how you are feeling right now. Fill in the blanks aloud:*
   - *"My body feels _____."*
   - *"I sense and feel _____."*
   - *"I notice my breath is _____."*

The Sound

2. *Take a normal inhale and then, as you exhale, create an elongated and soft "vuuu" sound . . . stay with this sound and sense into the vibration in the body that the sound creates. Notice how your body receives the sound.*

3. *Repeat the* vu *sound three times.*

4. *Now sense your body in stillness and open attention.*

5. *Fill in the blanks aloud:*

- *"My body feels _____."*

- *"I sense and feel _____."*

- *"I notice my breath is _____."*

REFLECTION

Discuss or invite the client to journal their responses to the following questions:

- What feels different now?

- How do you notice this **difference?**

- Where did you feel the vibration in your **body** by doing the sound?

- Can you still feel it now?

Breathing into the Central Channel for Balance (Wave Breath)

PURPOSE

In this exercise, your client will visualize an open channel like a vertical axis in the center of their body running from the crown of their head all the way to their pelvic floor. This practice is part of ancient meditation and martial arts traditions. It serves to ground and return the person to a sense of neutrality, equanimity, and spaciousness. This exercise can be very helpful when the client has experienced emotional dysregulation.

INSTRUCTIONS

This exercise requires sustained attention and an upright body position, such as a meditation posture. Provide a cushion or chair and ensure your client is able to sit for a few minutes. If they are in a chair, make sure their feet are planted on the ground. Then guide them through the following script:

1. *Close your eyes and draw your attention inward. Notice how you are feeling in your body. Fill in the blanks:*

   - *"I feel _____."*
   - *"I am aware of _____."*

2. *Imagine that there is a central channel that is running from the crown of your head down to the perineum, at the pelvic floor. This central channel is an open flow of energy running along your spine. There are no walls or boundaries to the central channel. You can imagine it as a soft beam of light or simply as an open, friendly space within the center of your body.*

3. *As you visualize the central channel, begin to feel the quality of your breathing rhythm. Imagine that your inhales and exhales are traveling inside the central channel like a big, slow-moving wave. This wave can travel with one inhale up toward the crown of your head, then down with the exhale into the pelvic floor. You can imagine the wave moving all the way up to the top and then down to the bottom again with a single breath cycle or, if it feels more comfortable, take your time letting your breath move gradually up and down the central channel like the tide rising and falling. Imagine that this wavelike breath travels within the central channel, bringing qualities of calm, centeredness, and ease.*

4. *Take your time as you're visualizing the wavelike breath traveling gently and slowly up and down the central channel to bring you peace and equanimity . . . then simply let go of your focus on breathing into the central channel. Return to a natural breathing rhythm and be fully aware of how you are in this present moment.*

REFLECTION

Afterward, have the client take a few moments to journal about how they are feeling in their body and mind after doing this exercise.

Sustained O Sound

PURPOSE

The O sound is primordial and can be heard in many styles of music and healing sounding traditions. It fosters deep inner states of relaxation and resonance. This exercise is helpful in modulating activated feelings. It can be soothing to start with this sound when there are sensations that are held or stuck in the body. If the client is self-conscious making the sound, you can mirror their sound to support them.

INSTRUCTIONS

Use the following script to guide your client:

1. *Start by taking a baseline of how you are feeling right now. Notice your breath quality.*

2. *Take a deep inhale and then, with the exhale, sustain a long, soft O sound. Rather than pushing the O sound out, see if you can bring it into your body. You might feel a vibration or resonance in your chest. Notice how this sound feels in your body.*

3. *Repeat this O sound a few times until you feel a vibrational movement in your body. It's easiest to feel it in the chest region. You can place one hand on your chest and imagine sounding into your hand.*

4. *Let your next inhale be natural and then, with the exhale, make the O sound as one long, sustained sound. Listen to the sound as you make it and feel your body in response.*

5. *Repeat this sound five times and then rest.*

6. *Now open your attention and sense into your body. What do you sense in your body right now? Has there been a shift inside? Notice what has changed and what is more available to you right now. Are there feelings of opening, softening, or ease?*

Humming into the Bones

PURPOSE

Humming is an ancient human sound. It is found in all cultures around the world, and it can be used to regulate any activated inner state. In this practice you will be directing the sound of humming into the bones of the body. Bones are filled with fluids, and the vibrations of humming can create inner resonant states that are very beneficial for toning the vagus nerve. It is ideal to introduce this as a guided exercise. After practicing in session, you may want to assign it as homework.

INSTRUCTIONS

This can be done while the client is lying down, reclined, or sitting up—whatever is comfortable for them. Guide them through the following script:

1. *Place your fingertips on your clavicle bone. Support your arms so that they are comfortable, since you will be in this posture for a while.*

2. *Start by inhaling deeply and then exhaling. Repeat three to four times to establish a connection with your body. Pay attention to how your body is feeling right now.*

3. *Then begin a gentle and sustained humming sound. You can explore and play with different sounds until you find a tone that you can repeat and deepen.*

4. *Focus your attention on your clavicle and your fingertips touching it. Send the next humming sound into that area. Imagine that your fingers are sending the sound into your bones and the humming is traveling throughout your skeleton. Humming sounds can have a texture of delicious, sweet, tender, or any other quality you would like to send to your body.*

5. *After three or four more humming sounds, take a rest. Return to a natural breathing rhythm and observe your body.*

6. *Repeat this cycle a few times until you feel the humming has created a shift.*

Listening to Sounds of Self-Compassion

PURPOSE

This is a helpful exercise to support the client in finding calming and compassionate sounds in their own body for self-regulation. It is effective even when large movements are not accessible. The vibration of one's voice is a subtle movement. The client both creates the sounds and receives them as a resonance in their body. For example, a low-pitched O sound can be felt in the belly or chest. Let this be a mindful exploration of what feels soothing and resonant. After you have guided the client through this practice, in which you will model the sounds, they can use the *Sounds of Self-Compassion* client handout that follows to practice outside of session.

INSTRUCTIONS

1. Explain to the client that sounds are movements we feel in the body, and this exercise will involve making soothing sounds and noticing what happens in their body.

2. Encourage the client to bring to mind an image of compassion that they will focus on as they receive the sounds, such as a kind, beloved person in their life. It should be an image that has meaning to the client. This helps them to be relaxed and receptive to hearing and making sounds into their body.

3. Explain that you will model different sounds for the client, which they can then try out for themselves. Let them know that their job is to receive the sounds and study the resonance and what happens in their body. You can say, *Focus on the sensations in your body and how it feels when you hear the different sounds. After you hear them all, pick one that you'd like to hear again. Then see how it resonates. You are looking for a sound that opens you to self-compassion and acceptance. Each person has a slight preference—explore what feels right to you.*

4. When you model the sounds, make them be low, soft, sustained, and with a long exhale. After you make each sound a couple of times, pause and invite the client to make the same sound. Have them use a lower tone of voice, allowing a slow breath and rhythm. Let there be no judgment, and invite them to take their time. The quality of the sound matters. You can say to your client, *Imagine you are delivering these sounds to a person in need of soothing.*

5. Use the following sequence of sounds. For each one, make the sound once or twice, pause, and then invite the client to repeat it.

   - *Hmmmm*

   - *Awwww*

   - *Ohhhh*

- *Tzzzzsss*

- *Yeaaaah*

6. After the sequence is complete, pause and invite the client to notice what is occurring in their inner experience. If there is a sound they prefer, invite them to repeat just that sound and see what this will evoke. If you notice any spontaneous movement, encourage the client to follow it.

REFLECTION

Provide paper or ensure your client has their journal, and ask them to draw whatever imagery came up as they listened to the sounds of compassion. They can also answer, "Where in your body did you feel these sounds?"

 CLIENT EXERCISE

Sounds of Self-Compassion

PURPOSE

This is a deeply nourishing practice that you can come back to whenever you need self-regulation. You will generate soothing sounds that are associated with compassion.

INSTRUCTIONS

1. Bring to mind an image that fills you with a sense of compassion, such as a kind person in your life, a beloved pet, or the feeling of being supported by the earth or warmed by sunshine. This can be anyone or anything that brings a feeling of compassion, kindness, or acceptance.

2. As you visualize this source of compassion, what sound comes to mind? For example, you might remember a time when this beloved figure was singing, humming, or speaking in a warm tone toward you. Remember the sound in your body and how it made you feel.

3. Now begin to make that sound and direct it into your body. It helps to go slowly, using a lower tone of voice and sustaining the sound so it resonates inside your body. Breathe in and then make the sound as you slowly exhale.

4. Take a breath cycle after making the sound. Rest and receive this sound, feeling the effects of the sound or the words that you're resonating with in this moment. Focus on the compassionate aspects of this sound and how your body begins to ease or relax with it.

5. Continue to make this soothing sound, pausing in between to notice your experience, for as long as it feels supportive for you. You can also explore different sounds to see if you prefer another one. Here are some soothing sounds you could try:

   - Hmmmm
   - Awwww
   - Ohhhh
   - Tzzzzsss
   - Yeaaaah

Micro-Movements

PURPOSE

Micro-movements are a very powerful way to increase the intrinsic awareness that the body *is* movement. Micro-movements lend themselves easily to working with any constriction, tightness, frozenness, or limitation in the body. They are intrinsic movements that don't require a lot of effort—in fact, the less effort your client puts in, the more benefits they will feel inside. Micro-movements are also helpful when your client doesn't feel like being expressive through large movements but still needs the benefits of feeling their moving body.

INSTRUCTIONS

Invite your client to get comfortable; they can sit, lie down, or stand for this exercise. Micro-movements can take some time to feel and sense, so you want your client to choose a body position that they can be in for a while. Then guide them through the following script:

1. *For this exercise you may like to close your eyes, if that feels comfortable for you, to sense into the tiny, subtle movements you will be making in your body.*

2. *Begin by sensing the tip of your nose. Draw tiny little circles with the tip of your nose, as if you're making a little drawing . . . then reverse the circle in the other direction . . . you can also draw a tiny figure eight with the tip of your nose.*

3. *Notice how the back of your neck begins to move and open up more sensations . . . now explore moving your neck without the awareness of the tip of your nose. Notice how the movement quality changes. Does it feel denser, or more willful, or more constricting?*

4. *Now come back to the tip of your nose and explore further, making tiny micro-movement circles and figure eights and noticing the fluidity of movement that begins on the back of the neck and upper thoracic spine.*

5. *Now that you have a feeling for how small and tiny micro-movements are, open up your awareness into your whole spine. Begin to move down the spine, making micro circular or angulating movements. You can travel up and down three or four vertebrae at the back of the neck, the thoracic spine, or the lower lumbar region. Find an area in the spine that's easily accessible to you.*

6. *Reduce the effort of the micro-movement—make it smaller and smaller until you feel a sense of fluidity and ease with the movement and the spine. Explore now how the micro-movements invite qualities of undulation in the spine.*

7. *Every now and then, take a deep breath.*

8. *Now, let go of any movement and simply notice as you stop moving how intrinsic the micro-movement has become. Does it feel like your body is moving by itself? You have now entered the terrain of the intrinsic micro-movements within your body.*

9. *Let these micro-movements wander up and down your spine for a few moments . . . and now let go of the initiating of the micro-movements. Take a deep breath, then exhale and receive the intrinsic movements that you're perceiving within your body. Notice how the micro-movements are opening up new somatic sensations within.*

10. *Now let your body come to complete stillness. Receive your body as it is right now in complete, open attention. How do you perceive yourself? What is different in your embodied experience?*

11. *Finally, change positions or open your eyes and notice if your perceptions have shifted.*

REFERENCES

For your convenience, purchasers can download and print the worksheets from this book at
pesipubs.com/traumasensitivemovement

Avila Gonzalez, C. A., Driscoll, M., Schleip, R., Wearing, S., Jacobson, E., Findley, T., & Klingler, W. (2018). Frontiers in fascia research. *Journal of Bodywork and Movement Therapies, 22*(4), 873–880. https://doi.org/10.1016/j.jbmt.2018.09.077

Bartel, L., & Mosabbir, A. (2021). Possible mechanisms for the effects of sound vibration on human health. *Healthcare, 9*(5), Article 597. https://doi.org/10.3390/healthcare9050597

Boehme, R., Hauser, S., Gerling, G. J., Heilig, M., & Olausson, H. (2019). Distinction of self-produced touch and social touch at cortical and spinal cord levels. *PNAS, 116*(6) 2290–2299. https://doi.org/10.1073/pnas.1816278116

Bryant, R. A. (2016). Social attachments and traumatic stress. *European Journal of Psychotraumatology, 7*(1). https://doi.org/10.3402/ejpt.v7.29065

Chikly, B., Roberts, P., & Quaghebeur, J. (2016). Primo vascular system: A unique biological system shifting a medical paradigm. *Journal of Osteopathic Medicine, 116*(1), 12–21. https://doi.org/10.7556/jaoa.2016.002

Chivukula, S., Zhang, C. Y., Aflalo, T., Jafari, M., Pejsa, K., Pouratian, N., & Andersen, R. A. (2021). Neural encoding of actual and imagined touch within human posterior parietal cortex. *eLife, 1*(10), Article e61646. https://doi.org/10.7554/eLife.61646

Friedman, D., Goldman, R., Stern, Y., & Brown, T. R. (2009). The brain's orienting response: An event-related functional magnetic resonance imaging investigation. *Human Brain Mapping, 30*(4),1144–1154. https://doi.org/10.1002/hbm.20587

Goldsby, T. L., & Goldsby, M. E. (2020). Eastern integrative medicine and ancient sound healing treatments for stress: Recent research advances. *Integrative Medicine, 19*(6), 24–30.

Jefferies, A. L., Canadian Paediatric Society, & Fetus and Newborn Committee. (2012). Kangaroo care for the preterm infant and family. *Paediatrics & Child Health, 17*(3):141–143. https://doi.org/10.1093/pch/17.3.141

Landis-Shack, N., Heinz, A. J., & Bonn-Miller, M. O. (2017). Music therapy for posttraumatic stress in adults: A theoretical review. *Psychomusicology, 27*(4), 334–342. https://doi.org/10.1037/pmu0000192

Metro Richmond Zoo. (2023, March 30). *Orangutan learns how to nurse from a breastfeeding zookeeper.* https://metrorichmondzoo.com/orangutan-learns-how-to-nurse-from-breastfeeding-zookeeper

Schultz, K., Cattaneo, L. B., Sabina, C., Brunner, L., Jackson, S., & Serrata, J. V. (2016). Key roles of community connectedness in healing from trauma. *Psychology of Violence, 6*(1), 42–48. https://doi.org/10.1037/vio0000025

Schwartz, A. B. (2016). Movement: How the brain communicates with the world. *Cell, 164*(6),1122–1135. https://doi.org/10.1016/j.cell.2016.02.038

Shafir, T. (2016). Using movement to regulate emotion: Neurophysiological findings and their application in psychotherapy. *Frontiers in Psychology, 7,* Article 1451. https://doi.org/10.3389/fpsyg.2016.01451

Sippel, L. M., Pietrzak, R. H., Charney, D. S., Mayes, L. C., & Southwick, S. M. (2015). How does social support enhance resilience in the trauma-exposed individual? *Ecology and Society, 20*(4). http://www.jstor.org/stable/26270277

Smith, S. M., & Vale, W. W. (2006). The role of the hypothalamic-pituitary-adrenal axis in neuroendocrine responses to stress. *Dialogues in Clinical Neuroscience, 8*(4), 383–395. https://doi.org/10.31887/DCNS.2006.8.4/ssmith

Sparling, J. W., Van Tol, J., & Chescheir, N. C. (1999). Fetal and neonatal hand movement. *Physical Therapy, 79*(1), 24–39. https://doi.org/10.1093/ptj/79.1.24

WHO Immediate KMC Study Group, Arya, S., Naburi, H., Kawaza, K., Newton, S., Anyabolu, C. H., Bergman, N., Rao, S. P. N., Mittal, P., Assenga, E., Gadama, L., Larsen-Reindorf, R., Kuti, O., Linnér, A., Yoshida, S., Chopra, N., Ngarina, M., Msusa, A. T., Boakye-Yiadom, A., . . . Massawe, A. (2021). Immediate "kangaroo mother care" and survival of infants with low birth weight. *New England Journal of Medicine, 384*(21), 2028–2038. https://doi.org/10.1056/NEJMoa2026486

ACKNOWLEDGMENTS

Movement is innate and yet we learn the art of movement from each other. I want to acknowledge my teachers Emilie Conrad and Susan Harper for teaching me the primordial depth of Continuum Movement. They have informed my life and somatic trauma teachings in profound ways. I have learned from Indigenous teachers, including griots of Senegal and Ghana, about ritual dance that grounded me into the earth. I learned to appreciate the mindful movements in relation to the natural environment from Suprapto in Java, Indonesia. The teachings of Contemplative movement practice from Barbara Dilley and Irini Rockwell taught me that space can be brought in between each moving breath. I learned from Janet Adler and Tina Stromsted in Authentic Movement how to witness and hold movement processes. In contact improvisation I learned the art of listening to another moving body and how to hold balance and gravity together. I learned to express emotions and imagery through dance art performance. Susan Aposhyan and Bonnie Bainbridge Cohen taught me about experiential anatomy and developmental movement sequences. Gabrielle Roth's movement work taught me about essential rhythms and community dancing. Anna and Daria Halprin taught me how to engage the expressive arts and moving body.

Many other wonderful teachers and communities influenced my moving body awareness and grew my understanding in how to facilitate and track movements in others. Much gratitude to my students and clients, who so bravely move their bodies to find their way through trauma imprints to their essential fluid selves. Lastly, the most profound movement teacher has been nature itself. Moving alongside rivers, among the trees, and by the oceans has taught me how to listen to my body in union with the natural world, to find my way back home.

And to the reader, a therapist's tip: Move, move, move—and it will show you the way.

ABOUT THE AUTHOR

Manuela Mischke-Reeds, MA, MFT, is an international teacher of somatic psychology, author, somatic trauma psychotherapist, and Continuum teacher. She co-founded the Hakomi Institute of California and Embodywise, a nonprofit educational institute that brings together the wisdom teachings for the body. She developed Innate Somatic Intelligence™ Trauma Therapy Approach (ISITTA), an in-depth training program for therapists and practitioners, integrating somatic trauma therapy and movement practices.

Manuela's background in movement and dance started early and has involved both formal training and informal practice, including ballet, modern dance, movement and dance therapy, African dance, and her immersive experiences moving in nature. She has studied contemplative dance in Indonesia, trained in Authentic Movement, trained with Emilie Conrad and Susan Harper in Continuum Movement®, and holds degrees in movement therapy studies from Naropa University and somatic psychology from California Institute of Integral Studies. She has bridged her movement training with her trauma studies, somatic psychology, and somatic meditation traditions. She has worked with a wide range of diverse clients and culturally diverse groups, finding creative and adaptive ways for all clients to relate to their moving bodies.

Manuela has over 25 years of clinical psychotherapy experience with diverse trauma clients. She lectures and trains professionals on the topics of somatic psychology, trauma therapy, embodied movement practices, and psychedelic-assisted therapy.

Manuela is the author of several books, including the *Somatic Psychotherapy Toolbox: 125 Worksheets and Exercises to Treat Trauma and Stress* (PESI, 2018) and *8 Keys to Practicing Mindfulness: Practical Strategies for Emotional Health and Well-Being* (W. W. Norton, 2015). Visit Embodywise.com or ManuelaMischkeReeds.com to learn more about her work.